T0078312

LIFE'S PUNCTUATED IMMORTALITY

ROBERT L. WOODS

ARCHWAY
PUBLISHING

Archway Publishing books may be ordered
through booksellers or by contacting:

Archway Publishing
1663 Liberty Drive
Bloomington, IN 47403
www.archwaypublishing.com
1 (888) 242-5904

Because of the dynamic nature of the Internet, any web addresses or
links contained in this book may have changed since publication and
may no longer be valid. The views expressed in this work are solely those
of the author and do not necessarily reflect the views of the publisher,
and the publisher hereby disclaims any responsibility for them.

Any people depicted in stock imagery provided by Thinkstock are
models, and such images are being used for illustrative purposes only.
Certain stock imagery © Thinkstock.

ISBN: 978-1-4808-2475-1 (sc)
ISBN: 978-1-4808-2476-8 (e)

Library of Congress Control Number: 2015919371

Print information available on the last page.

Archway Publishing rev. date: 3/09/2016

Inscribed to Professor Edward O. Wilson, Humanitarian,
Naturalist and Entomologist,
Harvard University

Contents

ENLIGHTENMENT OF MANKIND

PART ONE
THE DAWN OF MANKIND

PROLOGUE

Through nature's vastness must we seek a voice
Convincing to the egocentric mind,
Which queries our resourcefulness, and choice,
To unify a vision for mankind
Mid dreams to rise as gods, and live but blind
To loathsome, mortal plight before the sun,
With doctrine that intelligent designed
Was life, such that immutably we shun
Enlightenment through science from dawn of life begun.

THE DAWN OF MANKIND

Awake! Among the myriad tones of spring,
From muffled winds through swaying boughs of pine,
To shrills articulated on the wing;
Arise to sweet melodies that intertwine,
As pollinators seek the latticed vine,
Rhythmic with blossoms of exotic scent
Diffusing like song, as essences combine
With colors born of visions that present
Repristination of the winter tenement.

And folding mists, in shadowed expanse through air,
Are jeweled in amethyst before the sun
Which soars as vaporous as a dream, to flare
The azure realm with glorious day begun.
And blessed beneath pale heavens are roses spun
Monarchical in scintillating hues,
As life, in efflorescence, all as one,
Inspires the heart through grandeur to infuse,
Divine and beautiful, the guidance of the Muse.

Where far extend the plain and verdant hills,
The sculpted remnants of a glacial mould,
Upraised are trumpet-flowered daffodils
Sweeping through wind, in rhythmic clusters rolled.
Then sudden, with still and panoply of gold,
Quiescence pulses the path of destiny,
And beauty, balm, air, fragrance are extolled,
Outpouring as one ambrosial recipe
Which stirs the breath of spring, all redolent and free.

And cloud-strewn shadows darken the mood of day
From summit to declivity and dale,
And whirled in evanescence, they portray
A somber tone beneath the tenuous veil
Enfolding wide, till celestial lights regale
The eye as atmospheric shades erode;
And last! Sunbursts, like waterfalls, impale
Cascading canopies of oaks bestowed
Triumphantly through landscape's undulating mode.

And 'tis from Nature should motifs arise,
Encompassing diversity and fate;
All intertwined are life, lands, seas and skies,
With themes of evolution which narrate
Subsuming principles, to colligate
The instances of natural selection.
Neutrality and nature integrate
A universal pattern and connection
Mid carbon based life, interdependent in direction.

Through evolution nature shapes a home
Of earth with starry skies, as we engage
The gift of life and majesty to roam,
Discovering our identity, its age,
O'er vast upheaval through geologic stage;
Motifs of life, boundless inspire a hope
That knowledge would mollify instinctual rage:
As once, in dark, surviving did man grope;
Advancing now with reverence, we dignify and cope.

Images, the mythologic, iconic,
Drape constellations o'er their starry frocks
As heroes, gods, exotic beasts demonic,
Synchronize with biologic clocks
Or gales arising at the equinox;
Traversing the night, silent, they immerse
Themselves in astrologic paradox,
Through light rays, causal links, to intersperse
Teleologic notion in the universe.

Beyond the planets and our noble sun
Is order born from mass and energy;
And stars evolve when galaxies are spun
From out a thermonuclear debris
As gamma-ray bursts ignite the cosmic sea
Which, rippling on the fabric of spacetime,
Expands with fanciful diversity,
So lovely, vast, thematically sublime,
That glorious is man's portion of this paradigm!

The universe is mortal like all matter,
A gelid field[1] entrancingly imbued
With stars and interstellar gas, which scatter
Their cosmic splendor in vicissitude.
It speaks with life transformed through genes accrued:
And, in summation, all things may embrace
Profoundness and a sanctity, construed
As adding radiance to the deep of space,
A spiritual and scientific interface.

---

[1] Higgs field. Predicted from the "standard model" is the Higgs boson discovered in the Large Hadron Collider at Geneva. The Higgs boson (field) generates symmetry breaking and thus is the origin of mass of the quarks (i.e., the Higgs gives other particles their masses).

Tellurian aesthetics burgeons splendent
When civilization unifies mankind,
Whose ethos, dignified through art transcendent,
Would stabilize divergency of mind.
Yet wealth and aspiration, when combined,
May taint our durance forged of finite years;
For destiny outspreads toward stars enshrined
To mark immortal that which man reveres—
His vanity below, subdued though it appears.

Pulsating from the heart is born a vigor,
Rebirth beneath the sunbeams, to entice
The youthful paragon to o'ercome rigor
By surpassing doctrine and ritualistic vice;
Yet maturation wretched grieves the price
Of truth, discerned amidst that lofty height
Where sacrificial loss of paradise
Bears loneliness, relumed before the light,
And grief, distilled below, unto forbidding night.

War-ravaged lives may flounder on the wave
Which, breaking, quick dissolves a fleshy core,
And sands amid destruction mark the grave
Of mouldering realms and rudimentary lore;
Till last, erosion shapes a neutral shore
As history, nameless, scrolls upon the ocean,
Whose warmth had nurtured sentiency before
Upsurgence of the mortal theme Emotion,
Which, conquering land, spawned self-awareness and devotion.

Ambition seeks in stars an exalted perch,
Noble unto the night, a luminous kiss,
Which, mounting as passion, initiates a search
To validate how metamorphosis
Through spiritual genes, evolving as artifice,
Conferred survival, and biased cosmology:
Constrained by genetic codes, we reminisce
Of sacred and celestial unity,
Till reason based on evidence would set us free.

Through symmetry-breaking as a phase transition,
The ruptured vacuum primordial powered creation;
Such uniformity at parturition
Progressed toward richness, diverse proliferation,
And fundamental force extrapolation
Mid stellar radiance, catastrophic strewed
As galactic-wreathed, expansive conflagration:
The universe in fiery pulchritude
Cast light upon the orbs, where sentiment ensued.[2]

Life's narrative begins as one remembers,
With disposition altered by event,
And passion kindles, like the glow of embers,
Igniting identity, with sentiment
As aspiration or dreamy discontent—

---

[2] Prior to the birth of our universe, there was symmetrical radiation at the highest possible temperature (this enormous energy and symmetry holding all the forces of nature [electromagnetic force, strong nuclear force, weak nuclear force and the force of gravity] together as a single entity), evolving as a symmetry of nothingness until undergoing a spontaneous rupture (as the Big Bang), resulting in our visible universe which may progress to a distant future of radiation at the lowest temperature possible (black hole radiation, until they evaporate, followed by the Dark Era).

In shaping nature's realm, man is surpassed
By probability and accident;
Through dreams, contingencies illusive cast
Transcendence, ruled by nature, the grand iconoclast.

The Goldilocks phenomenon prevails,
Allowing evolution to progress;
A subtext to reality entails
An order, broadened through biofriendliness:
A cosmic code, stochastic, to express
Such fundamental laws: the theoretic
Alludes unto design, a grand largess
For sophistry, with patterns viewed prophetic
Toward a realm eternal, rational and aesthetic.

How blessed is fabled perpetuity,
That lingering morass of time and space, consigned
To self-awareness and its casuistry?
The mask of eternity leaves ill-defined,
Faint, vacuous, the visions of mankind
Who espies in utopia such timeless domain,
Beyond the slumber of death, though undermined
By finite sensory integration whose pain
As anguish, slays the heart, imprisoned and insane.

Imagine mythos, as computerized,
Merging with machine and mechanistic,
Conceiving a consciousness more synchronized:
Assimilation would be idealistic,
Algorithms for each characteristic;
With sensory input almost infinite,

Could man evolve, remaining optimistic
That, technologically, the benefit
Preserves our heritage, the human requisite?[3]

The forms most beautiful forever change,
Averting involution and despair,
And quantum fluctuations render strange,
Statistical configurations there
Within the brain or aptitude elsewhere,[4]
And superimposed environmental stress,
Acting synergistic, may impair
Adaptability and strength unless
The rate of change o'ercomes, a mechanized success.

With signals rippling o'er the brain's synapse,
Identity subsumes diverse allusion
Toward sense of self through neurologic maps,
Redundant circuits, matchless with inclusion
Of sentiment unique through varied profusion.
Synaptic rhythms, when compromised, may cross
Erratic through conscious voids or a contusion.
Could cultured stem cells compensate brain loss,
With metamorphosis of mind the albatross?

Mankind transcends as progeny of stars
Which beacon consciousness, with evolution
Of mind emergent from the brain, to parse

---

[3] As with many innovations, small steps allow for careful analysis and the ability to more adequately address mistakes and unanticipated results. Billions of years of life's evolution appear mechanistically to support man's need for a thorough understanding of biological as well as artificial intelligence, and to what extent each one would impact and possibly overtake the other.

[4] Quantum entanglement of consciousness and its persistence

Coherence in nature, and its contribution
Toward intelligence. Yet execution
Of merging mind and cosmos, with respect
To axiomatic schemes, bears institution
Of fundamental laws, which may project
A nanotechnologic buttressed intellect.

Across the universe in shockwaves and fire,
Exploding stars and supernovas yield
The birth of elements, from out the pyre,
Cloaking with destiny the nebular field;
And isles mid stellar genesis may shield
Life's resurrection, upon acceleration
Of cosmic expansion, that could distant wield
A fate of cold midst black hole radiation,
Or exponential death, the Big Rip termination.[5]

Mutability arrays all things
As interwoven, the simple to exotic,
With harmony that mathematic springs
From systems, deterministic yet chaotic,
And order, unifying and hypnotic
Should spacetime, supersymmetry align.
Though nature's laws, evolving, rule despotic,
A universe's death would undermine
The destiny of all, from cosmic to divine.

---

[5] It wasn't until 1998 that the universe was noted to be *accelerating* in its expansion based on observation of supernovas. If dark energy increases in value, ultimately the expansion of the universe would become superexponential to infinite, thereby rending everything from star clusters to atoms—the so called Big Rip (an end to space and time).

Is mathematics discovered or invented?
For every physical reality
There is equation, extrapolation presented,
As nature resonates with symmetry,
Laws codified, expressed numerically.
And all analysis and calculation,
Theoretic, elusive—could it be
Dark energy and matter's elucidation
Would caparison creation splendorous through unification?

Through man's repeated and inveterate fall,
'Tis with an isolated glimpse, we take
What solace lies in nothingness of all.
From quantum jitters does a cosmos shake
Into existence, only to forsake
A hope, a permanence, unto design
Where life, love, beauty eternal would awake.
And sweetest fruits spring from the withering vine
Like day most beautiful, contrasting in decline.

And hence, must love and spontaneity,
Intensifying, fall as sacrifice;
Transfiguration of life's imagery,
Through nature's order, changing, is the price
For consciousness, frontiers of paradise
That immortality would soon exhaust,
Despite a sophistry it might entice.
Life's equanimity is like the frost—
Fanciful, serene, and so easily lost.

We sing unto the universe our songs
Of human frailty, meagerness and loss
Amidst the superclustered-galactic throngs,

Creation's lights that massively emboss
Spacetime; and still our lives are not mere dross:
We are an ethos of eternity,
Placid in migratory pomp across
The bridge of imagination and destiny,
O'erlying the vast, divinely mirrored cosmic sea.[6]

Into the abyss of time, the night sky
Traces a lineage bound to a distant shore
Upon the void; a cosmic lullaby,
Sung there from infancy, would evermore
Resound toward self-awareness and outpour,
From primal-birth tones to intelligence,
That consummate leitmotiv, and deep restore
Life's fellowship, concordance, mid intense
Reflections toward legacy, and spiritual recompense.

We are the progeny of laws of nature,
The mathematic essence of a God,
Ruling by process or such nomenclature
As winter wind, rippling like a prod,
Freeing seeds, dehiscent from their pod,
Which lost, wavering unto the void of distance,
Are bound by nature, recondite and odd,
Which links transfiguration and existence
Through universal motifs, or mutable consistence.

There is a resolution for mankind
Through central, unified world government

---

[6] According to the WMAP (Wilkinson Microwave Anisotropy Probe), space is flat. However, it may not be infinite, but resemble a "hall of mirrors" with the illusion of distance based on various models of topology.

With church and state no longer intertwined.
Subsuming principles which represent
Sustainability would circumvent
Overpopulation, and counteract
Toxicity. And 'tis most evident
That evolution must be taught as fact,
And religious creed—genetically evolved extract.

Noontime passes while sodality
Is territorial on the tree and hill;
Stridulation echoes with harmony
From sylvan to campestral haunts and rill,
Where swift, a crackling bough induces still,
With quietude through broad expanse averred;
Then zephyrs, cadenced in airy swells, fulfill
A melody in reminiscence heard,
Inspired by tones embodied on the hummingbird.

Companionship extends through stately reaches,
From wave-swept shore to tempest-plaited peak,
As nature, bound by adaptation, teaches
Expressiveness from artistry, to wreak
Sublimity of beauty and mystique.
It is in man's discursiveness and place,
Mid mutability of life, to seek
Accord through nature's ancestry, and trace
Life's origin from Earth, or interstellar space.

As cloud-forms rise seraphic like a figment,
Aloft o'er heavenly sea they aggregate;
And time now spins the palette fashioning pigment,
Illusive and interwoven, to create
Motifs of passion, toweringly ornate,

Portrayals whose questing moods are emblematic
Of man outsoaring dark, to contemplate
A circumferential afterglow, ecstatic,
The light of vindication, transient, yet emphatic,

When swirling, clouds ascend the ethereal vault,
Fusing colors as though with angst distraught;
And all resolves, erratic, to exalt
An image writhing and fantastic wrought
As migratory bird, with pinions taut,
Enlarging, struggling on the clarion blue,
Till soaring high, emblazoned, with liberty sought
It billows midst a fiery rendezvous,
Transmogrifying into orbs with night's debut.

Unfurling lights intensify divine,
Phantasmagoric on the wave of dark;
And night-tide glitters as the anodyne
Of life, with soft and silver-splendorous arc
As equanimity surmounting cark.
And through augustness of the hemisphere,
All sentiments enchantingly embark
Upon extravaganza, to revere
Life's antecedents twinkling from a distant year.

Marmoreal whiteness images the Earth
Compassing the constellations bound
By a universe entropic since its birth.
And synchrony of systems most profound[7]
Creates a rhythmic order to propound—

---

[7] Cognition and self-awareness derive from the synergistic character
of nonlinear systems of order: an associated surge of neural (electrical)
synchrony.

That thoughts conceived, envisioned as volition,[8]
Are labyrinthine symbols which surround
Contingency[9] of cosmic acquisition
Inherent in the fire,[10] explosive toward cognition.

The deeper and more-fundamental laws
Reveal a statistic order to all things,
Evincing mankind's anthropocentric flaws,
And cast reality perchance in strings[11]
Or quantum gravity[12] as spacetime springs
Discrete, emergent in a causal way:
And godliness in nature spreads its wings,
As paradigms for self-awareness may
Immortal live in quantum fluctuant array.

---

[8] The illusion of free will.
[9] Recall exponential amplification known as the "butterfly effect," i.e., the sequence of antecedent states is unpredictable since small disturbances grow exponentially fast.
[10] The birth of the universe with the emergence of space and time.
[11] String theory and proposed multiple dimensions to nature.
[12] In the quantum theory of gravity, space as a continuum (i.e., the smoothness of space) is an illusion. It is postulated that space is made of discrete units (quanta) just as matter is made of discrete atoms.

Oscillating through eternity
Are ripples in creation's afterglow,[13]
Wherein primordial seeds of destiny,
Born of quantum fluctuations, grow
As galactic wreaths whose heavenly rays o'erflow
And pulse with stellar wind the astral zone,
Where rhythms of life and enlightenment bestow,
With light of dreams, a contemplative tone
Illuminating fate, amidst the dark unknown.

From dreams enfolded in quiescent mood,
To billows sounding through the tidal zone,
Are magnanimity, and fortitude,
Far-reaching in supernal overtone;
And loftiness binds notions which enthrone
The genesis of love, triumphant born
Unto the heart—as seeds are lightly sown,
And, burgeoning, in blossoms rich adorn
The sphere, which in its loveliness awaits the morn.

How lovely is the woven light of dawn
Harmonious with the heart's exultant glow;
How airy are the sunrays, arched and drawn
Prismatic, from the fiery orb below.
And colors blending with passion oft bestow
A rarefied awakening of mind,
Subsumed in heavenly artistry, to show

---

[13] The faint glow of radiation is the residual heat from the birth of the universe 13.82 billion years ago. The universe's large scale structure of galaxies, stars, planets, etc. was imprinted by quantum fluctuations during inflation. These seeds of large-scale structure are the hot and cold variations in the cosmic microwave background. The Planck spacecraft provided this thermal map of the sky at microwave frequencies.

How precious, how vast our lives are intertwined,
Ennobling unity, a vision for mankind,

Which dreamingly is cast as deep reflection
On life and all that is our privilege,
Through nature's isle, to find of such perfection;
We hold these values dear, so as to pledge
Our hearts, and memories, from which we dredge
The mortal tones that outward strike a chord,
And, in summation, lead unto the edge
Of ethos and expansiveness, explored
Through harmony of love: herein is our reward.

The wind arises like a theme ancestral,
In many voices cycling o'er the plain;
Melodious, the distant and orchestral
Marches resonate toward sighs in vain,
Departing, sounding till hush and loss remain;
And yet, through death is born tranquility,
Waking serene, contrasting as its reign
Yields last a rebirth gusting upon the lea,
Analogous to life, its punctuated tree.

Discovery as a process flourishes
When life, its pace, and progress, are endowed
With mutability which nourishes
Ideas, converging, enfolding like a cloud;
If veiled immortal—an indeterminate shroud.
Through death are fragmentation and surrender,
And seasons mantled with nothingness avowed,
Awaiting nature's path toward vigor, splendor,
Composite goals reconstitution would engender.

All things arose from one primordial fire

Uniting matter, energy and fate
Through laws of physics as celestial lyre,
Whose tones across the universe create
Motifs of liberty, and life elate
With love voluptuous strewn through cosmic sea:
Where all the strings impassioned resonate
Till dissonance concedes mortality,
And expiration sounds with nascent harmony.

Life, enfolded in love's sweetness, wakes
From dreams amid a lightsome, airy clime;
Then hushed, plutonian darkness swift o'ertakes
Refulgence pinnacled in thoughts sublime.
Perchance, based on a species paradigm,
Congruity unites, then reconciles
The loss that lineaments the face of time.
Through punctuated splendor, mankind styles
The star that reigns o'er immortality's dark isles.

The sun presides upon a blue pavilion,
Animating life whose purling stream
Is chambered, discrete as waves of rich vermilion,
And fused with colors quantized in a dream,
Encoding thought in holographic gleam;[14]
And consciousness emerges, volatile,
From quantum jitters to light sheets as a scheme,

---

[14] Dreams are believed to be internal holograms. The holographic principle asserts that information is imprinted on the event horizon of a black hole. Analogously, in our everyday world, a two dimensional surface, called a light sheet, encodes all the physics that compose it in three dimensions. The information contained on the surface of a light sheet is projected onto the three dimensional world, which is what we see. It is suspected that the light sheet gives rise to the fabric of spacetime—an emergent phenomenon.

Illusive and nonlocal, to beguile
The mind's reality, which time must reconcile.

Phantasmal are the visions interfused
With perturbation of the waves of sleep,
Like dreams tumultuous from a mind contused,
Bizarre in rhythm, which conjures from the deep
The specter death, on fiery steed, to reap
From life its harvest flaming through fields infernal;
And clouds, ignited with lightning streaks, sweep
In conflagration over skies nocturnal,
And thunderous wanes the trance, toward wakefulness diurnal.

As stygian cloudscapes interweave a sadness,
The weltering heart, o'ercome by teardrops, falls
Turbulent bound unto the depths of madness,
Whose torrent with a tempestuous efflux sprawls,
O'erwhelming hope, as storms, and violent squalls,
Invidious deluge sanity with wrath;
And tragedy transfixing life appalls
Perception, paleolithic bound as path
Of natural selection's internal conflict aftermath.[15]

Throughout a calm, the fruits of nature perish

---

[15] After millions of years as hunter-gatherers, sedentism did not occur until about 15,000 years ago (slightly antedating farming and domestication of animals).

However, genetic adaptations which served us well at the egalitarian hunter-gatherer stage, later manifested as barriers toward unification. When exceeding a group of approximately 150 individuals, instability involves hierarchies in aspects of government and economies, overall resulting in tribal conflict.

Charles Darwin referred to our prehuman and Paleolithic eras as the "indelible stamp of our lowly origin."

When cankerous grows the tree from tainted seed,
With vigor, once bountiful and sound to cherish,
Eclipsed harsh by the pestilential weed;
And light, though radiant o'er azure fields, would bleed
With coldness through an atmospheric veil.
Yet, as the Tree of Life again is freed,
Outstretching boughs and strength prodigious fail,
For shallow cling the roots to life's eroded trail.

The chasm deep within, where dwells despair,
Enlarges as the Tree of Knowledge grows,
Luxuriant robed, deceptive in its snare
Of lengthening shadows cast to augment woes.
Yet cultures anguished, lost to wisdom, close
The paths that compromises oft entail,
As insurrection, rending the heart's repose,
Plunges communities into travail
Till blind, relentless, they the global realm assail.

Diplomacy is foreign to the heart;
It breathes not passion, from life eulogized
Or leavened with nature's glory, to impart
Resounding dreams o'er past idealized,
And neutral, shuns a future polarized
By visions of uncertainty and woe.
It flows, within the moment, dichotomized:
Though virgin streams from youth resplendent glow,
The tortuous waves through time create life's bright sunbow.

As youth recedes unto the fleeting years
Enfolded in eternity, we grieve
Alone for consolation through frontiers
Where time and veneration would retrieve
A vision of self, enduring, to conceive:
Transcending o'er these evanescent hours
Is faith, distilled like balm from summer's eve,
As starry isles expand and fragrant flowers
Entrance our world with love, in dew-suspended showers.

And sudden, the spell is broken by a truth,
Founded on reason, seizing life's embrace
Of homocentric voids, the maze of youth;
And such entrenchments, if unchecked, deface
Subsuming principles which interlace
Neutrality and nature, the symbolic
Methodology of time and space.
Amid our thoughts, sublime or melancholic,
Is mythologic veil illusionary frolic.[16]

From consciousness and privilege are meaning,
Centrality and free will but illusion;
Through mind, and nature's laws supervening,
Is neurologic mapping an inclusion
Of memory and images, in fusion
With flow of time, illusive and emergent,
Conferring survival, strengthened by intrusion
Of purpose in a universe divergent
From destiny, as man's reflective self resurgent.

---

[16] Incorporated in the neurobiology of the brain over the course of evolution is the essence of neurotheology, which genetically involves all cultures, having served initially as an adaptive, cohesive survival mechanism.

As quantum eternity explosive shattered,
A multiverse of fire configured morn,
With vestiges, the universes scattered,
Reflecting, from separate laws of physics born,
Such fabled conformations—vast, time-worn
By exotic metamorphoses: and one,
Unique, through inflation's[17] void had shorn,
And streamed in galactic splendor with a sun
Neath which a blue-green world of self-awareness spun,

For space and time were unified as day,
Crystalline, divine o'er Earth's domain
Evolving toward life, which through its gladsome lay
Shone light upon lush fields to ascertain
The rhythm of the ocean and the rain,
Rebounding in cycles, replenishing the sphere,
Melodic as the pulse of eve's refrain
Cadenced above, a vaulted chandelier
Of starlight infusing into the essence of life's cheer.

Enlightenment must serve this pristine world,
Cataclysmic flung from cosmic flame,
Refining, what geologic time unfurled,
A fragile self-awareness which o'ercame
By random process, blindly, as to frame
An altruistic bond: 'tis man's decision,
Clothed in dreamlike majesty, to claim
A guardianship sustaining long-term vision.
Our species holds potential, yet dallies in derision.

---

[17] In the very early universe, symmetry breaking occurred, resulting in phase transition and release of energy that expanded (inflated) the universe by a catastrophic factor. Hence, the visible universe is but a fraction of the entire universe since inflation far exceeded the speed of light.

Proliferation free from spoliation;
This neutral creed mankind must not exceed,
With integration short of usurpation,
As strength, dominion lead not unto greed;
And balanced through equality, we heed
A thankfulness without idolatry:
Adorned through beauty, may aesthetics breed
A joyous process of discovery
Unto this punctuated immortality.

Controversy underlies pragmatic
Assertion, as life's presence frames abysmal
Constraints on evolution through erratic-
Cosmic conditions, initial, paroxysmal;
For nature's laws, fine-tuned, set cataclysmal
Restrictions. The universe, kaleidoscopic
Born, diverse-inhabited, casts prismal
Splendor on man's observations—a topic
For premise of existence, the principle anthropic.

Manifestations of reality
Are images imperfect, vague, distorted,
The pixels in the portrait of destiny.
Through mankind's mirror, with curvature contorted
In still more asymmetric guise, is purported
Insight presaging and deceptive: 'tis curious
That through reflection enlightenment is thwarted,
As that illusive and outspreading spurious
Becomes a pragmatism, mystic and injurious.

Religion reigns intense among the masses,
Unchanged in ideology through time,
And strangely moves some educated classes
Dogmatically constrained upon their climb,
The rites of passage to a fate sublime.
And wars have roiled amid religious scourge,
Whose depredations vastly mark the crime
Against mankind, as doctrines cannot merge,
And life denuded falls, unable to converge.

While mythical viewing the zenith's azured haze,
Grandiose we pause through brief sojourn,
Splendored in glory, till departing rays
Evanesce beyond the twilight bourne,
With night's embroidered stars to vain discern
As relic orbs that reify our sorrow:
Divine, the light o'er time would cloy, as we yearn
After the unattainable, and borrow
Such vision as man's fate, uncertain unto morrow.

Destruction of the ecosystem bears
War's signature through quietude and peace;
Extinction flourishes as man forswears
His link with nature, squandering in caprice,
As though such plight would harbor no release
From misery, scorning a straitened world effaced
By profiteering. Supremacy will cease
When overpopulation has outpaced
Life's equilibrium, and man has shrunk abased.

Man's exploitation fosters no relief;
Compulsive drives ingloriously endorse
And magnify the manacles of grief:
Festering o'er time, pervasive is remorse
That tensions billow with unbalanced force:
In youth, disguised as innocence and wonder,
This unrestrained, magisterial source
Mounts fear, titanic as the thrust of thunder—
Sequela from the strike, intense as mankind's plunder.

A festering wound may on the surface scar,
Disfigured deep in agony and ire,
And aspiration, like a shooting star,
Would fall unto the night and then expire.
Besieged with pain, the form upon the pyre
Awaits as vengefully emotions quake:
Intense and feverish, fulminant with fire,
Convulsing through the body they o'ertake
The equanimity, which would upheaval slake.

And malediction rankles in the mind
As empires seethe, imperialistic bound,
With desecration wrought and man maligned;
And gasping deep, a phantom Earth is crowned
With fires, the volcanic nightmares that vile redound
To sovereigns, whose blaze-born shadows rapaciously
Race into nothingness on barren ground,
Uniting in conflagration o'er the sea
Where clamorous fold the depths, in vain cacophony.

Will winter veil the spring in dreamless sleep,
From day and night-scape smoldered into one?
Will frozen be the tears forlorn to weep,
With love, all vanquished, ceased before the sun?
Man's plight, in mythologic shroud begun,
Found war as destined animus from the start;
As such, would Earth's funereal firestorms, run
By mankind's mystic and unstable heart,
Portend the fate of life through universe apart?

EPILOGUE

The birth of universes may progress
Toward cosmic natural selection's end,[18]
As shattering the symmetry of nothingness
Yields nature's laws, evolving, to transcend
The dark when constellated stars resplend.[19]
And born of stellar remnants is a theme
Of life, transfigured through time to comprehend
How godliness may rise in nature's scheme
Of physics unified, the quintessential dream.[20]

---

[18] The "seeding" of daughter universes analogous to Darwinian natural selection.

[19] The expanding universe, its laws of physics and evolution of life and self-awareness arose from the Big Bang [i.e., the broken primordial symmetry of nothingness (a vacuum as quantum landscape out of which a universe(s) is born)].

[20] The visionary splendor across the universe derives from motifs of transmutation. Auspiciously as forebears, stars light the galactic wreath with a dynamic force of life. As one entity entwined in this punctuated immortality, we as humans struggle to define a destiny. Perhaps we triumph when aspirations are warmed by the phantasmal fire of dreams. What follows is a creative efflorescence as enlightenment is guided by compassion.

ENLIGHTENMENT OF MANKIND

PART TWO
THE CORONATION OF MANKIND

Tranquility belies a turbulence
Mid stars with planetary realms that hath
A violent birth, progression with intense
Geographic shift along the path
Of plate tectonics, quakes, volcanic wrath,
Neath comets, asteroids, that searing plunge
With shock waves and a fiery aftermath,
Till starry transmutations, upsurging, lunge
Across the solar systems, and carbon life expunge.

With time and fate entwined, despite explosion
Or violent upheaval, life would persevere
Through atmospheric changes, storms, erosion,
Or social evolution to adhere
Toward balance in aesthetics and the sphere
Of scientific inquiry, with quest
For legacy, in spite of zones austere;

Such that migration is the manifest
Survival for a species, an interstellar guest.[21]

Behold the enigma of eternity—
As virtual particles whose evanescence
Through quantum fields drives vacuum energy.
And once, a replicator forged the essence
Of life-forms, mutable, with adolescence
Conceived of sentiency; and such fruition,
Woven from starry fields of incandescence,
Evolved through time a consciousness, ambition,
Discerning nature's realm, though fused with superstition.

The face of reality is but illusion,
A sensory cloak, apart from nature's laws,
Projected, underscoring man's conclusion
That self-awareness triumphs as a cause
Internalized, though wretched with innate flaws:
Purpose, anthropocentric themes sophistic
Rule. And yet, neutrality withdraws
Such universe designed for man, where mystic
Move the gods concealed, arcane and casuistic.

Triumph extends unto imagination
Diverse as waves, expansive, vast and free,
Lashing the shores in rage and desperation;
The search for truth is veiled in tyranny
Of thought, which resonates rhapsodically,
And rare with heavenly laws would synchronize:

---

[21] Migration has alleviated stress in regard to increase in population, warfare, resources, xenophobia and divisive religious indoctrination (tribalism).

Certainly, migration's genetic roots will culminate initially in robotic exploration of the nearest stars.

Yet observation adds a vital key
To access nature's levels of disguise,
Transcending doctrine's void, and all man prophesies.

Plutonian Earthscapes dark with desolation
And cloud-forms shadowed in premonition recede,
Yielding a starry salience whose gyration
Derives from galaxies that fiery speed
Across the cosmos—pinwheels in stampede
Outshining by supernova explosiveness.
And neutron stars and pulsars violent breed
Black holes, warping spacetime to coalesce
An event horizon, as holographic surfaced recess.

The mood has changed, and shooting stars through dark
Expand with moonbeams splendorous in their rise,
Evoking majestic birth, the matriarch
Of all the universe, which glorifies
Expressiveness mid landforms, seas and skies,
As meaning through the cosmos rules iconic
When introspection, percipience, comprise
Its rhythms, periodic and harmonic,
Contrasted by motifs of origins symphonic.

Pulsing through solitude, cascading falls
Gleam amid the glory of starlight;
A voice, commanded by the wind, recalls
How water and the elements unite,
And intricate the rhythms of life excite:
With carbon-bonded macromolecules
In veiled and random process, recondite,
Deciphered through quantum physics and gene pools,
A replicator acts, and animation rules.

The night-tide quivers in a phantasy,
With dreams transmuted into talismanic
Airs of enlightenment, before they flee
The psyche, vacillating from brief panic
To equivocal quiescence; thoughts galvanic
Race throughout the spurious, scientific,
And fusing, presage among the stars titanic
Beauty and visions—a universe prolific,
Momentous in meditation, mid darkness soporific.

How privileged we are with self-awareness,
To momentary glean the cosmic splendor
As part of visions, doubts and thoughts of fairness,
Of how the human species may engender
A code of ethics, and historic render
Our consummation—carbon based, which cast
Unto the void of time and space, would tender
Ethos and quintessence of our past
And future legacies, should dreams survive steadfast.

Serene upon the deep is morn's repose
Amid pavilioned hues: a vast auroral
Awakening configures to a rose,
Prismatic and stratifying o'er seas in floral
Sublimity. Contrasted are the coral
Reefs, that luminous submerged appear,
Reflecting the heavenly temperament's restoral
Of vision, diurnal varied, to endear
Diversity of life, its changing biosphere.

Beyond the horizon, a sulphureous morn
Bursts from its heavenly chasm, intense, thematic
Of genesis, as ambrosial light is born.

And spun in vaporous splendor, homeostatic
Is life, whose sun, through nuclear fusion, emphatic
And diaphanous flares toward a path extinct:
Yet life and legacy may change erratic,
Deriving laws of physics—entangled, linked,
To metamorphosis, from distant realms in sync.[22]

Revitalizing patterns of abstraction
Sculpture beauty as a panoply,
Mystifying through its rarefaction,
And vivid in color and refulgency—
Like rainbows coupled, ascendant o'er the lea,
Inscrutable within the atmospheric
Moods of nature whose soliloquy
Divulges the auroras, and esoteric
Coherence of all things, illusive and chimeric.

The beautiful transcends through exaltation,
Frolicsome as waves that lift aesthetic
Vision, and mutable with animation,
Accelerating as it grows frenetic,
Intertwining, noble and poetic:
And images outspreading exponential
Cast themes of life, ascending, energetic,
That spin the galactic wreaths with vast potential,
Transfigured by contemplation and a love essential.

---

[22] Extending from physics to the origin of life, the rhythms of nature have had a profound tendency to synchronize, resulting in a self-organized (spontaneous) order in the universe, derived from chaos. This underlies modern complexity theory, particularly the subjective experiences of consciousness, self-awareness and the illusion of free will.

When passions from aesthetics merge with science,
And light the torches of eternity,
Such theoretic and divine alliance,
Galactic caparisoned, uprises free,
Relativistic, quantized by decree;
Through multiple dimensions, all upheaval
Reveals consecutive topology:
Inflationary sequence with retrieval,
Propagates through cycles, budding as primeval.[23]

Suspended in a sunlit trance is Earth,
Radiant with swirling seas of bright sapphire
And cerulean skies, etched with clouds, mid birth
Of wind songs, trills from birds; a celestial choir
Streams ethereal o'er nature's vast empire,
Profound and interwoven with dreams, ambition,
In apotheosis, to inspire
Summation of man's cosmic voyage and mission,
Till mortal tones recede, extinguishing cognition.

Mortality allows mankind to measure
How time and aspiration symbiotic
Flourish, assimilating unto pleasure.
And destiny, however vast, exotic,

---

[23] This topology is applied to the multiverse which theoretically is infinite in its array of universes, each with random laws of physics. Hence, most universes would be sterile, although some may harbor life, such as our universe with carbon based life forms. The mechanism by which the multiverse spawns universes is called eternal inflation. New universes are born (budded) out of inflating space, analogous to soap bubbles in a bath. Thus, there are endless cycles of birth (budding) and death (retrieval) in the multi-dimensional matrix of general relativity and quantum mechanics, where matter and energy are interconvertible.

From nanotechnologic to robotic,
Must pause; for resurrection of its light,
Once fallen unto life forms when aquatic,
Will rise with stars. Through paradigmatic plight,
Renewed and self-aware, shall life conceive insight.

Through quantum-relativistic realms of forever,
Our punctuated immortality,
As carbon based motifs, would random endeavor
To organize, defining such chemistry
As unifying, self-aware and free,
Within the life-span of a universe,
To light the galactic whorls with destiny—
Of life recasting genomes as to rehearse
Transfigurations, which rippling o'er waves of thought, disperse

Surpassing the stochastic with intention:
Ideas transcend, arising meteoric,
Encompassing the cosmic-veiled dimension
Through artistic prowess, summations oratoric,
Vibrant in metaphor and phantasmagoric,
Like supernovas explosive in star shower,
With nature radiant, resounding and euphoric:
Such themes of life, evolving, shall empower
Spacetime with rationale, deep within its bower!

When love of life glorifies aesthetics,
That leitmotiv eternal is conveyed
And personalized through probing of genetics,
With nuances of carbon realms arrayed
And eulogized as meaning, love portrayed
Cyclic midst a fragile corridor
Across dimension, where dreamingly remade
Are lyrics strange, familiar to outpour:
"And I have loved you ever, and will forever more!"

LOVE'S AWAKENING

A haze receding tenuous through air,
Like a specter fades. And veiled sunrise
Is jeweled amidst the clouds: a solitaire
Intensifying, glowing, sears the skies,
And compassing the zenith would symbolize
Love's consummation—thematic from the heart
Which pulsates picturesque and multiplies
The rhythmic refinement toward a new day's start;
And, binding with light of heaven, life's tenor does impart.

And love's inconstant airs, exalted, light,
Harmonize the odyssey of spring
When modulations rippling through wind excite
Romance, and melodies upon the wing:
For life mid providence and sun would sing
In exultation, rendering seasonal mood
Like a lute, fine-tuned, in which each string
Conveys tonalities of gratitude
Resonant of love and tranquil interlude.

RAINBOW

Color and contemplation are transfigured by romance
When passion blossoms upon the atmosphere all tinctured
    divine.
And rarefied, reflected, visionary forms entrance
Perception, as symmetry and radiance distant intertwine,
Till vaporous born across the firmament such bright rainbows
Palatial, in spectral luminescence transcend the vast cosmos.

The wave of color binds our sentiments before it fades.
For each emotion, is a subtlety in hue expressed,
And through life's noble journey, may we add these tints and
    shades
To vivid cast a rainbow in prismatic lightbeams blessed.
Ephemeral are the tones of life bestowed on halcyon skies,
When heralded by the rainbow arched above its golden eyes.

SUNBOW

Along the torrent's perpendicular,
Enfolding through vapors, rises a bright sunbow:
Imbued with passion, this myriad-beamed lodestar
Of vigor, reflecting like an afterglow,
Airy spans the azure undertow;
And dividing in radiance, ever soaring higher,
A polychromatic archipelago
Islanded by water and light and fire,
Dissolves through mists in a trancelike, soporific gyre.

Upsurging with the sunbow, is contemplation
Forceful, impassioned in primeval splendor
As colors changing hue shape inspiration—
Oft serene, immeasurable and tender,
Or spiritual with a vision to engender
Beauty, expansiveness, divine as sun
Enrobed in meridian majesty, to render
A consummation of colors and moods when spun
As life's rich sunbow, whose tones harmonic blend as one.

Illusions of light and shadow link these falls
With nuances of texture, exotic arrayed
O'er crevices of weathered rocks and walls,
Arching and curling the streams; a glistening cascade
Submerges in seraphic grandeur toward shade.
And morning haze precipitates as dews
Glassed upon the towering palisade
Whose vast reflection of heavenly realms renews
Phantasmal dreams of love, mystic among the hues.

NORDIC SUMMER

The hues of heaven enfold on glacial tiers
In iced serenity from summer clime,
Whose glow through arctic midnight perseveres
Profuse with splendor born in nature's prime,
And wafted through nocturnal fields of time.
Transcendently is beauty veiled, like dreams,
O'erspreading images of life sublime
Which, glassed within the purity of streams,
Find tones of passion opalescent in sunbeams.

The fjords and skies are mirrored in deep marine,
And islanded by clouds which buoyant sweep
O'er rocks and matrices of mountains green,
Precipitous above the fathomless deep
Where shadows interfuse, cascading steep
From palisades amid the silver height.
And flowers entranced with dews and fragrance weep;
Yet unto morn a love may blooms requite
While blessed by breezes drying tears with soft delight.

How stately glows the Scandinavian sun;
Steadfast, the imagery intensifies
Boundless from out a landscape intricate spun
Of nature's moods, that mingling, harmonize
Tranquility across cerulean skies
With lyricism upon the wave's domain—
While themes unveiled by man would eulogize
Refulgence o'er mountain, lake and field of grain,
Divine vouchsafed of love, and cleansed by wind and rain.

Mid spaciousness does solitude bear truth,
A comfort through the lone, and mechanistic,
Observation defining mankind's youth.
Derived from love, with passions idealistic,
Contrasting is maturation, whose artistic
Motifs are moored by wisdom to the shore
Of discovery—moulded by the synergistic
Interplay of inspiration, and lore,
Exuberant with life, though humbling evermore.

Where days must yield to dark, there is illusion
When solar wind impacts with gaseous glow;
Auroral luminescence prompts suffusion
As arcs fantastically entwined o'erflow,
And shimmering sprays and waterfalls bestow
A visionary kingdom in the night,
With vaporous stairways serpentined below.
Effaced by morn, the realm of folding light
Departs with stars suspended in diurnal flight.

DAFFODILS

Spring awakens mid the daffodils
Upraised through tufts of snow or icy grass,
Quaffing mists the atmosphere instills
As morning breaks its slumber o'er the morass.
Undulating trumpets of gold and brass
Glorious ignite the fields through nature's bowers,
Where bright with sunbeams they expansive pass
In luminous beauty which like a dream empowers
Rejuvenation of spring, glossed by seasonal showers.

Through gusting wind, sequential wave-forms ripple
In harmony, a leitmotif of spring;
Till sudden, in quiescence they brightly stipple
The vales and hills and rocks to which they cling.
Above, is melody upon the wing
As festive, birds broadcast their mating songs:
Through the trees or open air they sing,
Or roving far, triangled rise the throngs
Soaring o'er daffodils; elsewhere the heart belongs.

As clouds recede, the sunbeams rich suffuse
The daffodils with radiance below.
Outspread, diversifying color renews
Phantasmal fire and rapture they bestow
To life, land, air and season's scenario,
When lyrical, reflecting o'er the sea
Or imaged in rathe hues of skies aglow.
Tempered by time and mutability,
Contrasting is a loveliness upon the lea.

And protean is life through climate change.
When fragrant blossoms yield their sustenance,
Each pollinator finds its ideal range;
Yet niches vary, and rhythmic like a dance,
Environmental nuances and chance
Rhapsodic march o'er nature's promenade,
Inconstant modifying each expanse.
Evolved through time, the daffodil's crusade
Encompasses mutation, survival's masquerade.

The daffodils of many moods entwined
And metamorphosed neath cerulean skies,
Tincture light of dreams across the mind,
A rarefied, prismatic paradise.
All fanciful does musing mobilize,
When phantasy, exotic configured instills,
Mid sanctity of sun and butterflies,
Fathomless auras, as afterglow o'erspills
Tinting cognition cast amid the daffodils.

SEARCH FOR DEFINITION

Palisades when sculpted of rock that towers
Lofty toward heavens, the pristine, azure recesses
Of sanctity adorning nature's bowers,
Are met with wind, whose paroxysm caresses
Flocculent clouds with overflowing tresses
Rippling o'er pools, the mirrors of the glade.
Each image cast by nature evanesces
As time, erosion, in metrical cascade
Improvise with rhythms, a worldly serenade.

Islanded through fields, gold daffodils
Maturing, image the sun's angelic light;
And undulant o'er greenery and hills,
They greet the bees and butterflies in flight.
Life's cadences, complexity invite
Subsumption under motifs as to revere
A periodicity, and shrewd insight
Into man's place amid the Earth's frontier,
With safeguard of its vision, the fragile biosphere.

The search for definition must begin
With introspection, discovering midst all things
Equality, when unified as kin.
Through balance, nature in concordance sings
Of interdependence, as tenuous life clings,
Evolving o'er time by natural selection.
From science, aesthetics, identity upsprings
Intensified by cosmic interconnection
As stellar death seeds life, a starry resurrection.

The challenges of life define man's goals
Tempered with magnanimity from dreams.
Imagination, the lodestar within, extols
Vicissitudes of phantasy. Sunbeams
Combine with flow of consciousness which streams
Divergent in thought, mood, philosophic refrain,
As biodiversity expands its themes.
And illusive light of love may bright sustain
Life's unity, renewal, and ethics more humane.

LOVE

A sweetness dallies in the starlit air
Woven of nature's musings to impart
An integrated love, lustrous, fair
With thoughts perspicuous from out the heart
Splendid veiled with passion's stately art
Outpouring in swells, like moonbeams through a cloud
Or shadows unfurling in mystical upstart.
And love with energetic verses vowed
Reigns fanciful and free, and dreamingly endowed.

A music kindled by waves across the sea,
Folds in many modulated scales
As rhythms harmonize afar, carefree,
Across spumescence tempered by winds and gales.
Exotic assembled, replete with themes, love hails
Sublimity along the open shore,
Where life o'er land pursued time's distant trails
Transitioned from waters and leading unto lore
Enriched by love's aesthetic pathways to explore.

And tenderly, beneath the stars, alone
She listens as the light intensifies,
Caressing white lacework imaged first in stone.
A cadence through the night-tide prophesies
Ethereal tones, uplifting, to galvanize
Her heart into the blessing of desire;
Till radiant, her flaxen hair and azure eyes
Portray with splendor a story to transpire,
Enraptured of life and love, the strains of nature's lyre.

BEAUTY

Incisive clarity of facial features
Transfigured by a symmetry sublime,
Resounds with harmony mid nature's creatures,
Impassioned, beautiful—a noble prime.
And vivid color intensifies o'er time,
Binding a leitmotif which picturesque,
Through artistry exotic in paradigm
Aggrandizing creation's arabesque,
Arises with emotion, profound and statuesque.

Expression is a universal veil,
A modulation within, refined, urbane,
Woven of passion, love, in rich detail:
Melodious as the metric pulse of rain
Outspreading far, till waves of softer strain
Lavish distill in dawn's angelic light.
Such atmospheric dreams and blessings humane
Integrate, upspringing into flight
Unto aesthetic bliss, all beautiful and bright.

LIGHT

Serene and still, angelic spreads the light
Luminous beyond where radiant glows
The rising orb of day, all mystic bright
And veiled in clouds. A nebulous repose
Dissolves across the horizon as splendor o'erflows
Expansive, beautiful. Enchanting it streams
Casting the glory of distant-strewn rainbows,
As colors interfuse and august sunbeams
Mingle with the mists and illusive light of dreams.

With clearing skies, the light upon the ocean
Sparkles on wavelets mid the aquamarine,
Enfolding, reflecting, magical in motion.
From waters to heavens, sunbeams crystalline
Unite the majesty of Earth pristine,
With noon changing toward eve in starry array
Which twinkles through night's inscrutable ravine.
'Tis light transfiguring diurnal paths of day
As beauty blossoms o'er land amid a floral bouquet.

ROSE

Soft, outspreading light of dawn
Intensifies to veil the rose,
Resplendent as a cabochon
Which, faceted by petals, glows.
Placid neath the skies, while glassed in dews,
A tenderness, and love of life, the rose renews.

Elegant, in bright pastels,
The blossoms, exotic textured, stream
Cascading, arching o'er walls in swells,
Interwoven like a dream
With images, the tapestry sublime,
Profuse, phantasmagoric in the lush springtime.

The glossy leaves are dense, reflective
Of morning sun as blossoms twine,
With canopies of color perspective
Diverse, majestic in design.
Harmonious arrayed, the cycles of bloom
Adorn the hillsides, plains, and many motifs assume.

Through fragrances, bouquets impart
The auras of emotions bound,
Deep recessed, within the heart;
Yet sentiments unleashed, profound
As love, are interlinking like the rose—
Each added like a petal, life's story would compose.

SPRINGTIME

Bright hues restore the moods of spring,
Outspread mesmerically through air
When birds enraptured on the wing
In revelry o'ercome despair
From winter chill. Such liberation
Pristine with love greets all creation.

Ephemeral blossoms of pale cerise
Distend, filling with beams of light,
Till toppled by wind and honeybees
Releasing auras, a springtime rite.
From field to canopy, perfume
Airy ignites the mystic bloom.

Spring's majesty, monarchal fashioned
With colors vibrant o'er land and streams,
Reflects in waters such moods impassioned
With atmospheric cheer of dreams—
A springtime eulogy mid skies
Woven of wind and butterflies.

ATMOSPHERE

The light of heaven, fluctuating, sprawls
Angled through clouds as a bright sunburst
Diffuse with sprays amassed as waterfalls
Streaming angelic, distant, till immersed
In colors, rarefied and interspersed
With haze, fine rain all mystically entwined,
Receding toward the horizon, then traversed
By interlacing cloud-forms, wispy, aligned
With tones of azure muted, contrastingly combined.

And sunrays permeate the wood and veiled
Leaf fenestrations, illuminating glade,
Cascading falls with sunbows rich detailed.
And far, the atmosphere is vast arrayed
In grandeur, lofty o'er the palisade,
Boundless diffusing unto heaven's domain.
From Earth to sky are visions oft portrayed
As mutable as dreams, with bold refrain
Of atmospheric color, or monochromatic rain.

BY THE OCEAN AS MORN AWAKENS

Starshine islanded o'er galactic dark,
Scintillates where constellations had scrolled.
And faintest azure sculptures the skyward arc,
Uplifting morning dreams with visions of old,
Diaphanous through mists where hues that bold
And dithyrambic transfigure the depths of eve.
And seashores afar, imaged with motes of gold
Sparkle through morn, like stars that gently upheave
Across the cosmos, dissolving o'er paths they interweave.

Billowing fires ignite the dawn at sea
As distant, color harmonies arise
From sky to lyrical beyond the lea;
While interwoven as a paradise,
Diverse wave-forms, cloud-veils romanticize
The drama of nature, bound by radiant sun
Volatile, mutable, amid a guise
Of atmospheric phantasy when spun
From meridian heights, prismatic to rainbows rich begun.

COMMUNION AT SEA

A cloud-veiled luminescence spans the wave
While winds uplift our vessel from the shore;
And rhythmic through vast ocean-spray we brave
The swells accelerating mid a roar
Of waters ghostly crested, lashing free
Till formless in the firmament of night,
Where stars are clustering, and rotate toward the sea,
Sparkling as spumescent lathered light.
And through the mists a sanctity unveils
Mid glow impalpable as light of dreams;
For visionary illusion fancifully hails
From tidal distortion, chaotic neath moonbeams.
And homeward bound, we glide toward sandy dunes,
Reposed o'er spreading sea where life communes.

RAIN

Through stately pines tumescent clouds of gray,
Contrastingly, subdue the light of day,
And sprinkled on a silver morn is rain,
Placid, hushed, expansive o'er the plain,
Where not a piping from a lonesome bird
Or whisper from the forest can be heard.
Quietude sustains ethereal peace,
Though light and shadow mingle in caprice,
Tempting a shrouded sun to shine once more
On waters clustering, defining a primal shore.
And nature's harmony is like the mind,
Whose thoughts o'erflowing soothingly unwind
And join the rhythm of hypnotic rain,
Wherein the pulse of life bears its refrain.

FOG I

Stratified, o'erlying trees and mountains,
Are cloud-forms burnishing a dim pathway,
Tenuous as mists o'er salient fountains
Whose vapors uplifted are tinged by light of day
Till radiant born sunbows have arched o'er spray.
Expansive, the fog delineates a theme
Of somber beauty, a mystical array;
Or nebulous would soft portray a dream
Tranquil, showered in mists that monochromatic stream.

And fog intensifies beyond the dawn
With warmth, convection, circulating breeze,
The rhythms of condensation as to spawn
Atmospheric illusions, which by degrees
Entwine, transcendent layered o'er water and trees.
And yet, ephemeral recedes such revelation
Of nature. Haziness, wind, phantasies
Contrasting, veil light-beams—a consummation
Phantasmagoric reminiscent of creation.

FOG II

Obscuring tree-line, mountain and winding stream,
The forest darkens, vaporous mantled by fog.
Decanting toward valleys, scrims of mist and steam
Distend as condensation o'er sea, marsh, bog,
Composing, in silence, the new day's brief eclogue
Of pastoral beauty. Such atmospheric dance
Is slow in procession; a barometric cog,
Balanced by wind and warming, alters advance
Sustained by rhythms innate, across a vast expanse.

Tenebrous, opaque in stolid tones
Enfolded, a leaden semblance lingers as haze,
Till zephyrs, circulating, disperse through zones
With clearing meadows, dells and waterways:
And sifted through cloudscape, soft, the first sunrays,
Intermingling in nature's drama, blend
With fancy, choreographing aerial ballets
Improvised, as hues with shadows contend.
And harmonized by heavens, celestial lights transcend.

CELESTIAL LIGHTS

The afterglow dissolves toward light of dreams
As soft, the setting sun trancelike streams
Amid its colors, reflecting, and bestows
A luster, in pastels, which overflows
Unto the sky's meridian deep, where veiled
As phantasms, images diversify
Exotic, vast, extravagant detailed,
Fusing effulgence as to prophesy
Utopian visions, fancifully entwined
To move with color the matrix of the mind.

Serene, the heavens resplend unto the night
As wavelets curl with monochromatic light.
A soft breeze rustles through the canopy
Of conifers, extending toward the lea—
Mantled with blossoms in divine array,
Redolent of fragrance drifting far
Beyond the landscape; 'tis a spacious bouquet
In pale illumination from each star
Which twinkling, glorifies a galactic veil
Constellated across eternity's trail.

STARSHINE

The night's galactic veil of stars reveals
Diversity and order unto man,
As kindredly the heart with reverence feels
The glow from whence our destiny began.
Descended like an undulant illusion
Are folding lights transfigured on the wave,
Cresting, curling and falling in perfusion,
While echoes through the wind evoke a stave,
Lively, lyric and lifted by the sea.
Beyond the shore and silhouetted hills
And redolence of jasmine o'er the lea,
There stirs a phantasy which oft instills
The sentiment to fancy things divine —
When night is woven in a starry trance,
The visions of creation intertwine
And bind the universe's broad expanse.
And love of life escorts us through the dark
Dissolved as morn, divinest clothed of hue
Enriching dreams ascendant o'er the arc
Toward stars infused within a heavenly blue.

SNOWFALL

Uprising wind and clouds of gray
Contrast in phantom-veiled array,
Impassioned through winter chill.
And shadows stretching from land to sea
Distort the trees and imagery
Till sudden, all is still.

Inscrutable quiescence, bound
As frozen visage of air and ground,
Recedes before the sky,
When soft, amid ethereal heights
Tempered by haze and heavenly lights,
The snowfall drifts awry.

And poignancy and starkness change
As snowflakes, sculpting, distant range—
A renascence cloaked in white.
Such dreamy vision born aglow
Obscures reality's tableau,
Uncertain in its plight.

A harmony within dramatic
Stirs the heart, relentless, emphatic
Pursuing ennobled ends.
Yet snowfall like a phantasy
Exalts life's rhythms, bold and free,
As serene our love transcends.

RHYTHMS OF LIFE

Flowers cascade in color, with pollinator
Unique, evolved o'er time to probe each hue,
As plant or aerial emancipator
Returns the favor of a rendezvous;
Mutualistic sequenced, each aroma
Coincides with subtlety of chroma.

Ancient rhythms and a leitmotif
With variations orchestrate the dance
Above rare blossoms or round the cloverleaf
Till spinning, oscillating in a trance,
O'erwhelmed by pollen and exotic perfume,
Each creature rests, sheltered on the bloom.

And fields of floral beauty lightly sway
Mid breezes frolicsome neath morning sun
Girt by azure, spangling in gold array
Enfolded canopies all vaporous spun.
And freshness stirs from out the shadowy mist
Transfigured by sunbeams into amethyst.

This glorious day shall pass, yet be recalled
As rhythms of life unite in harmony.
Exhilaration leaves the heart enthralled
With beauty, divine outspread, rapturous, free,
Majestic in hues emblazoned o'er the mead
Enfolding in sequences to veil the seed.

ANNIVERSARY

Our anniversary, the hearts' renewal
Of love, ideals, and maturation veiled
Resplendent as the sparkle of a jewel,
Time's prism, the diamond intricate detailed,
Transcends voluptuous in emotions hailed
As celebration: a messianic bliss
Ensues, encompassing each mind regaled
By springtime resurrection and a kiss,
The union of two lives, born to reminisce.

In soft pastels, emblazoned is the dawn
Burnished like the contour of a bloom;
While billowy skies create the cabochon
Till cloud-forms facet azure and illume
The heavens in circlets, jewels that bright assume
Celestial harmony, which evanescent
Glows of love, aloft the morning brume
And sea, reflecting colors opalescent
On this day revered, exalted and quiescent.

Our anniversary becomes a part
Of rituals triumphant for mankind;
'Tis rapture metrical within the heart,
Outpouring in motifs so rare, refined,
Thematic blending legacy enshrined
In sentiment. And though our time recedes,
Leaving tonalities for life behind,
Matchless is the overtone which leads
Rebirth of lyricism, which love forever breeds.

DESTINY

The sifting of sunbeams from enfolded leaves
Toward wavelets glittering, wind-rippled o'er the sea,
Reveals motifs whose rhythm warm conceives
The light, mercurial strains of destiny,
Airy, entwining like a filigree
To unify the pathways of all things.
Such modulations blend as melody
Which, interwoven with dreams, pellucid sings
Of nature's panegyric: inspired the heart upsprings.

Transfigured by the pageantry of day
Is love, intoned in atmospheric bliss,
And rich adorning like a floral bouquet
In colors, moods with sweetness of a kiss,
And all ethereal from which to reminisce,
Eulogizing mankind's leitmotif
Across a scintillating starry abyss
Toward dawn effulgent on the new born leaf;
'Tis vindication, freedom, past the realm of grief.

DRAGONFLY

Forward and backward and whirling in arcs,
The dragonfly soars and airy embarks
Hovering o'er land, dashing through skies,
The bliss of a heavenly paradise.

Chromatic in hue and reflecting afar,
It pulses the eye like the blink of a star,
Wandering, searching voluminous space
Where destiny conjures a wing-woven race.

Then sudden, it plunges toward aqueous domain
Hurling below like a wind-driven rain;
Or ascending o'er high iridescent aglow,
The dragonfly traces an arching sunbow.

Aerodynamic, exuberant in flight
Mid radiance spun from a vaporous sunlight,
Angelic as dreams on a soft, silver morn
The dragonfly streams as a vision airborne.

BUTTERFLY

Mutable in hues, a butterfly
Capricious as the wind encircling, calling,
Solitary drifts o'er fields awry;
And spiring in luminescence, mystic, enthralling,
Through fragrances hypnotic, it nears the bay
Undulant toward wavelets and sea spray.

Lavish, flung enraptured on the wing
Or cloaked above the mead in search of nectar,
The butterfly may spangle bright in spring
Or fluttering, diaphanous appear a specter:
This vision, like its metamorphosis,
Transmogrifies into an air of bliss.

The clouds and atmospheric garniture,
Amid the breezes, linger with light rain
Which tenebrous would life and sun obscure,
While misted monochromatic above the plain.
Yet far, the heavens divide, and rays dispersed
Like harp strings shimmer as a bright sunburst.

A path inspired by harmony of flight
From the pale azure toward the land and sea,
Extends unto all things; 'tis grand insight
Derived from nature's laws—neutrality
Subsumed in visions fair and mutable
As butterflies—rare, fantastical.

DEATH OF OUR BOSTON

(ADOPTED RACING GREYHOUND)

When nurtured moments with our pet depart,
Memories illuminate the love we find
Ecstatic woven, rhythmic through the heart
Awakened o'er time with myriad thoughts entwined.

His essence reigns as radiant as morning sun,
Expansive as the wind and floral mystique,
A majesty of nature intricate spun
From out its forces, subsumed in patterns unique.

And love in its meridian had graced our home
Consummating paths unveiled ahead:
When summoned by wind, rekindled, he would roam
Upon the night or where the moonbeams spread.

Such moments shared engender inspiration
And ethos encompassing eternity
As enlightenment derives from celebration
Beyond the starlight, infinite and free.

STARS

Twinkling modulation of the stars
Gyres within the waters still and clear,
As galactic rhythms revealed in night's memoirs,
Configuring modes of time and space, appear
Constellated as icons cavalier.
With birth of stars, a nebula empowers
Renewal, veiled beyond the atmosphere
Light-years away, contrasting with meteor showers
Departing as tracery, from out their fiery bowers.

Expansive is the mind profoundly tinctured
By apprehension of our origin
From stars, resplendent o'er the cosmos, cinctured
By night. And spiritual themes may underpin
An evolution, beauteous of life and kin,
Mutable across the universe.
Or resonant, uprising is the din
Of laws of physics to mathematic disperse
The music of the spheres, which life-forms would rehearse.

However glows the beauty of cognition
In myriad constructs sapient, cast serene,
Eternal is man grateful in his mission,
Beneath the azure, mid the evergreen,
Entranced by flowers or ocean's rippling sheen,
Unrestrained through nature's repertoire.
And ineffably conceived of night pristine,
Dwelt insurmountable its worlds afar
Till imaged, when extrasolar transits dimmed their star!

CLOCKS

A home replete with rooms has many voices,
The clocks that stand alone or grace the walls.
Diverse, each pitch melodically rejoices
In tonal modulation, and recalls
How spectrum of emotion resonates
Through time, partitioned mid spacious halls and gates.

Contrasting is tolling, alternate with ringing,
Or drawing chamber mellowed by a chime.
Consoling, tonalities may swell through singing
Or striking of bells, indicating time.
And sundials gauge the light across the sky
Where planets, asteroids and comets fly.

Though atmospheric veiled, the starlight twinkles
In sequences upon the Milky Way,
Until the dawn, pulsing in sunbeams, sprinkles
Metrical, expansive in array.
And time kept intimate within the home,
Transcends like dreams beyond the heavenly dome.

And in the vanguard, the pulsating heart
Is central as humanity's timepiece,
Contractible with chambers to impart
Stability as rhythmic its tones release
The leitmotif of love, ascendant, free,
Resounding through time, the pulse of destiny!

ETERNITY

'Tis mutability that binds all things;
Its voice, when modulated, mellifluous sings
Of Earth, sun, rain, wind, storm and atmosphere
Or Earth, crust, mantle, magma, sea frontier;
Such metamorphoses, tectonic forces,
Are cyclic neath a star which, pulsing, courses
Around the center of a galaxy,
The black hole tempest of eternity.

The cosmos through spacetime, expanding, wreathes;
Harmonic with the galaxies, it breathes
Stochastic, through a quantum mechanic veil,
Or relativistic on a larger scale;
And shrouded by dark energy and matter,
Acceleration, intensifying, may shatter
Galactic scaffolds, disrupting synchrony
Of space and time within eternity.

Humanity must celebrate its realm
As life unique upon the cosmic helm.
Arisen from out the sea in sunshine fair,
Evolving forms, entwined, and self-aware
Sang amid the splendor, in exultation,
Or wept before the rain, in consolation.
The forces moulding love and destiny
Evolve, while towering through eternity.

LEGACY

The ocean in its vastness acclimates
The sphere, neath sunrays glistening toward the lea;
And life, so splendorous varied in its traits
Originated single-celled at sea,
Rebounding through wave-forms rising, falling free
And hoisted o'er rocks till lost upon the shore,
Mid Earthscape's monumental pedigree
Of volcanism, its shifting reservoir,
With land tectonic rent, where rolls a strong temblor.

And colors exalt our sentiments, and cast
Idyllic beauty o'er land, sea, atmosphere,
As glaciers from the tinted peaks contrast
With sunbows misted o'er the falls' frontier;
Or aquamarine of ocean rippling clear
Is mirrored toward sky in crystalline array;
Till mutably, would azure domains inhere
In spectrum of moods, from dawn to close of day,
With colors passioned regal, evanescing to gray.

'Tis through the essence of our planetary
Sphere, we value life and consolation
Dear. And perseverance, patience, ferry
Dreams across the mind's phantasmal station,
Which moulds a self-awareness and causation
From laws of nature, evolving as emotion,
Intertwined and bound with all creation.
Fragile, mutable and born mid ocean,
Legacy prevails as wisdom and devotion.

HARMONY

The solar system, from an accretion disk,
Swirled, igniting the sun through motifs stochastic
As turbulent would nascent planets whisk
Through space and time. And man, iconoclastic
Rose, pondering forces, quantized, fantastic
Ruling along with relativistic laws,
Mathematic surmounting ecclesiastic
Doctrine conjoined with anthropocentric cause:
And life, from evolution, natural selection, draws.

The Earth, tempestuous born, with harmony
Cadenced by wind, fire, wave and aftershock,
Distorted by sun and moon through gravity,
Portrays equilibration like a clock
With periodicity through each epoch
Modulated, from sea and atmosphere
To churning, enfolding, of mantle's liquid rock:
And eccentricity and tilt uprear
With axial precession, altering Earth's frontier.

O'er geologic time, life-forms at sea
Diversified, adapting to land, till brief
Mankind unveils a sense of destiny
Through scientific insight, conquering grief
Imposed by dogma, obdurate belief.
Intense, aesthetic processes of thought
Have harmonized the science with leitmotif
Encompassing the stars, whose light beams taught
Of life's transfiguration, divine, poetic wrought.

MODULATION

The intertwining wrath of nature's forces
Across the sky, rebounding periodic,
Fluctuates in mood as it courses
With lightning prongs and thunderous motifs spasmodic,
Repeating, maniacal and flashed rhapsodic,
Forming with fiery incandescence a dance,
Metrical in anguish, as monodic
The winds and waters clash toward eerie chants,
When rhythm and rain combine, a modulated trance.

Music of madness rages o'er the mountains
Scoured by rock, ravine, frenetic light
Whose coruscations upsurge volcanic, like fountains
In phantom leap, filling the chasm of night
Fantastical and free; 'tis like a blight
Upon life's drama, dysrhythmic seeking peace
Mid stormy convulsion. Such atmospheric flight,
Explosive in sound and sight, is nature's caprice,
Erratic, insatiable, awaiting eruptive release.

The tones of nature, tempestuous in swells,
Reveal man's inner turmoil as ambition—
Beyond the edge of sanity it dwells
Shadowy, gliding like an apparition
Ill-constrained, eccentric in cognition.
And destiny assumes from nature's mood
Internal strife, the forces of sedition
That storm the psyche in verisimilitude,
Wherein a truth prevails, mid turbulence subdued.

TRANSITION

Seraphic lights create the afterglow,
A mingled reflectivity and burst
Of radiances, suffusing to bestow
Divinity—adrift the azure, dispersed
By clouds, which billowing transcend, immersed
Within immensity of twilight's veil:
Reservoired, the colors entwine, traversed
By deeper hues and shadows that mystic trail
As evanescences; rarefied they pale.

Textured by wind and mist, the folding sky
Hazed in soft pastels subtends a height,
Imaged as floral majesty o'er high;
Till last, the tones recede, and rich starlight
Colors eve in monochromatic white.
Contrasting with silhouettes, a full moon rises,
As cloudless skies intensify the night
Beyond an afterglow that symbolizes
Transition toward dark, arrayed in phantasy's disguises.

The dark portrays a calm neutrality,
Serene, uniting the starscape's lovely field
Of stippled light across the cosmic sea.
Yet 'tis reality with face concealed
By night; for distant in time and space, revealed
As residual radiation, a birthing zone
Was quantum induced—creation's background shield,
Whose microwave-veiled frequencies enthrone
Spacetime and genesis, the cosmic egg's birthstone.

NATURE OF REALITY

Observation leads toward evidence
To unify the natural world in thought
With random, neutral and statistic sense
Linking reality to forces sought
And codified through mathematics wrought
Of theory, testable, explanatory
Encompassing infinity to nought.
On probability rests nature's story
Deceptive unto man's religious veiled vainglory.

Science, as self-correcting paradigm,
Evolves through inquiry, dissent and cause
Experimental modified o'er time;
And ethics supervening then withdraws
Genetic spawned subversive rites and flaws
Comprising faith, indoctrination, blame—
Religious thralldom vitiates natural laws:
Since Gods evolved within a genetic mosaic,
O'er time, their mythic realms grew fancifully archaic.

WAR

'Twas during a unicellular evolution
That organisms met criteria for war;
And weapons, diverse in form and distribution,
Carved ecologic niches, a reservoir
Of nutrients and mates o'er vast seafloor
To land; such specialization drives conquest.
And life, including man as predator,
Has roiled amid diversity, obsessed
With power, dominion, rank, a genetic spawned contest.

Because warfare is deep ingrained o'er time,
Religious and politically its flames,
Like empires, rise and fall to veil the crime
Of retribution—thoughtless as one blames
A monarch, or reciprocally defames
His neighbor. Compliance, in vain, mankind enforces,
Though internecine struggle quick reclaims
The progress of humanity, and courses
Aggressive and altruistic in battles for resources.

Biologic change could close the schism
Among the realms with arms race and oppression.
Compassion intertwined with pacifism,
Awaits a unifying gene expression
Through sequences alone or in succession.
And yet, direct genetic intervention
May risk intensifying man's aggression.
Myriad factors underlie world tension
Until stability would rule through comprehension.

MYSTIQUE WITHIN

The blossoming fields define a rhythmic portion
Of nature's magnitude as winds enfold
And liberate the flowers in fiery distortion,
Contrasting with a viridescence. Gold
Mid rose, white, aqua tinting are extolled
And harmonized amid the blue serene
As birds in migratory waveforms hold
Communion where the seashores serpentine
Through beauty so bountiful, emotions intervene.

Sentiments augmented from primordial
Configuration, majestic forged a mind
Of visionary grandeur, since exordial
Musing in its dawn. And thus enshrined
Is man when love's motifs are rich defined
By Elysian splendor within, where efflorescence
Of aspiration is rarefied, combined
With pulsing of innate fire, whose vaporous candescence
Illuminates mystique, the heart's inspired quintessence.

CONFIGURATION

As sunrise veils a starry canopy,
The colors born of virgin day impart
A strength in songbirds, who find melody
To vivify the triumph of nature's art.

Through crystalline embrace of azure sky,
Triangled in migration distant bound
O'er land and sea in undulation high,
The multitudes with vibrancy resound.

Modulated are tones dispersing heard
Through cyclic gusts of wind across the plain,
Rebounding fervent from heavens administered
As nature's temperament to ascertain.

Life's harmony, ephemeral as a dream,
Transcends, evolved of rhythmic configuration;
And oft rhapsodic, in swells, subsumes a theme,
All mutable—cadenced as creation!

A CHILD IS BORN

Exhilaration exalts this lovely day
When glorious, a child is born unto the world
Blessed by light of heaven in gold array
As clouds recede with azure bright unfurled;
And nature, all versatile, awakens with life
From stream, land, air to iridescent height,
Harmonious in a celebration rife
With diurnal pulse of passion and delight;
While here this heart expansive claims its place
Where sing the seas bursting with ancestry,
O'erflowing fields alive with each embrace
Of sentiment to span eternity.

THE ROAD BEYOND

Glorious birth! A life is introduced
To self-awareness and heavenly light diffused
Upon a path, simple, of trial and error:
And, if obscured, a glance behind toward fairer
Thoughts, more certain, is like a memory
Secured with passion, the essence of emotion
Expressing paradigmatic identity.
The heart dynamic pulsates with devotion
Amid the dreams from family and friends,
As the road beyond in sunshine wends.

And knowledge ramifies into insight
Celebrating divine the morning light,
Soft and tranquil, from the orb of day
Guided by nature's laws. A vast array
Of stars transfigures the galactic zone:
Contingency for life intensifies
Beyond the Earthly splendor; 'tis unknown,
Apart from carbon, what life-forms comprise.
Ennobled through discovery, technique transcends
As the road beyond uncertain wends.

As acquisition, leadership progress
With maturation tempering life's success,
There looms ambivalence aloft a void
From loss and insignificance, which cloyed
With diffidence, create such overtones
Thematic of failure. Dismal, 'tis like a yoke,

Regressive and monotonous it drones
And yet, o'er time, would strength within evoke
A healing, whose enlightenment transcends
As the road beyond the darkness wends.

And wisdom, garnered from long years defined
By science, aesthetics, unifies mankind:
The universe from human intuition
Derives a self-awareness, a cognition
Subsumed by love into a leitmotif,
Radiant like the orbs, with harmony
Across spacetime, ethereal, o'ercoming grief,
Perchance with faith intoned to some degree.
Each life on self-reliant themes depends
As the road beyond inspiring wends.

ETERNAL PATH

Eternal path of mutability,
Across a radiant orb like Earth sublime,
Extends preserved, portrayed as memory,
Oft with introspection, paradigm
For love, subsumed within the heart o'er time;
Or vast transfigured, it versatile, afar,
Unites with dreams that atmospheric climb
Beyond infinitude, toward reservoir
Where thought transcends, impassioned, and rises with a star.

Through self-discovery and legacy, we learn
Of tones ephemeral, mortal bound as art
And music mid orient sun, with brief sojourn
Defined by nature; all things must depart:
Our lives and thoughts most dear unto the heart,
Like the universe grow old and die.
And yet through loss, upspring renewal, restart
Of self-awareness, punctuated by
Time's veil: therein a cosmic fate we may espy.

Exchange a glance for Earthly altruism
Or skyward, glimpse a visionary dream.
Imagination glides with lyricism
As thoughts enlightened, resplendent, radiant stream
In elaborate succession unto the rich sunbeam,
Tincturing the heavens like gemstone to immerse
The azure, rose and crimson color scheme
Mid fires of love, that roiling intersperse
Man's quests as tapestry across the universe.

Unrivalled color exalts the atmosphere
Though shadows, intensifying, create a mood
That somber, pulsing in loneliness austere,
Transmogrifies into an interlude
Of love forever lost—'tis solitude
Usurped by night in monochromatic array,
Perceived eternal dark. And 'twould denude
The psyche should regressive thoughts inveigh
Against love's resurrection, unsung and cast away.

This life, all momentary, is reconfigured,
Recast dramatic in motifs and splendor,
As geologic time, genetic triggered
Events and probability would render
A living paradigm with species gender:
Ourselves amid a different circumstance
Evolved with consciousness, emotions tender,
Through Darwinian natural selection, chance
And alien cosmic veil, the essence of romance.

WATERFALL

O'er waterfall collapsing through a mist,
Phantasmal gleam the sunbow's many hues:
Rising ephemeral, expansive the air is kissed
By a soft radiance that dreamingly imbues
The atmosphere with love as colors diffuse.
Rejuvenation finds its sentiment
Cascading like the waters, and renews
The blessings of these moments that accent
And purify life's springs—the heart they orient.

Rebounding falls cluster toward a pool
Calm, reflective of the morning haze,
Azure-blushed and stirred by winds that rule
Above a nebulous void, the zenith's maze
Of cloudscapes veiling sapphire-tinged sunrays
Streaming in glory like a cataract,
Till water and light dissolve, ascending in sprays—
Magical when liquid beams refract
Or blend unto the heart, whose rhythms interact.

I love this life in all its beauty bound
With passion, spiraled across the cosmic sea
Where nebulas, exploding stars resound
Toward themes of life, rising refreshed and free
From the still waters in gentle bonhomie.
I love this knowledge shared unto mankind,
Surmounting a void within our frailty,
With matter, life and energy entwined—
Rippling as motifs, a loveliness defined.

WATER LILIES

Near shallow waters and banks of inland ponds,
Reside the palms and ferns whose patulous fronds
Uplift unto the heavens in symmetry,
Arched o'er flowers strewn upon the lea;
And through the calm, reflective spaciousness,
From out the shoreline water lilies float
Entangled; rings of green leaves coalesce,
And blossoms distending free, the sunbeams coat,
Diffuse, in luminescence soft and pure;
Through photosynthesis, the plants mature.

Amid the leaves, cleft and richly veined,
On twisted rootstocks, flowers are maintained
As stellate, solitary whorls, aglow
With centers whose bright pastels profuse o'erflow,
And fragrances through wind uprise, ascending
Toward a veil, the stream of morning mist
That greets the sun, whose fiery rays extending,
Atmospheric blend in amethyst.
And water lilies in bountiful expanse
And colors, spawn an aura of romance.

Contrasting is the aerial water lotus;
Suspended above, pollinators notice
The myriad blooms, as petals bright effuse
Resplendence, whorled and born of many hues,
Mid shield-like leaves, and seed pods funnel shaped,
Swaying in wind, a rite before the sun.

And clustering leaves are intertwined and draped
All nebulous where shadows protean
Dwell mystic neath the sacred lotus rife
With themes symbolic of perpetual life.

Diversity of hues, miraculous born
To flowers in succession, arrays the morn
Whose energetic moods, divine inspired
Through azure heights, mingle with thoughts acquired
As a new day diaphanous through mist,
And radiant with sun, contrasting aerial scheme,
All beautiful, ethereal, is softly kissed
By loveliness, which vast configures a theme
Born of color harmony and light
Which water lilies with lyricism requite.

FIRESIDE

Round sizzling wood, the feathery flames, ascending,
Interweave in many colors, from blue
O'er ash to yellowed tips, airy, which blending
With shadows, flicker toward the chimney flue:
The ghostly apparel, of smoke and vapor, whines;
And seething, crepitant bursts of flaming coals,
Extruded o'er hearth, expire; the light defines
An atmosphere whose radiance consoles.
O'erspreading through darkness, 'tis a warming glaze
Of tenderness from out the logs ablaze.

Contemplation streams amid the glow
And quiescence, unifying from times passed
The memories, adventures, that bestow
Upon the night a loftiness. And cast
From out the flames, like an apparition,
Shadows distend on walls, writhing free.
Our gift of life, expressive in disposition,
Tempers dreams with light of phantasy
Rich as fiery candescence o'er the room,
And unto all a passion would relume.

SPRING

The windswept cloudscapes splendorous in portrayal
Of change, transition o'er the hills and vale,
Unmask sunbeams, encompassing the morn
In loveliness and revelry reborn.
The airy landscape glistens from the dews
Suspended, reflecting o'er flowers and ornament,
As rarefied the colors interfuse,
With fragrances as wind enhanced accent.
And perched o'er lavish beauty, songbirds rejoice
Melodic cloaked as springtime's lovely voice.

The cycles of bloom and atmospheric bliss
Mature, as boundless inspired, we reminisce
Revitalized and free. Life's pulses sound,
Intermingling, as memories rebound.
The songs revering spring's extravaganza
Requite these blessings, lyrical enshrining
Conciliation; bountiful each stanza
Uplifts, in exaltation, a love refining
Ideals from daily plight—which evanescent
Finds repose neath stars, in thoughts quiescent.

TEMPEST

The night diverges from a starry cope
Scintillating in sublimity;
Shadows stirring, in flight beyond a slope,
Are engulfed by tenuous light o'er eastern sea.
As tides are swept by wind and moon,
There lifts a leaden calm through copse
Rippling within a clear lagoon;
Above, the cloud-forms interweave,
Accelerating o'er tree tops
As geologic forces vast upheave
Creating a tempest lowering, concealed by shadowy eve.

Contrasting is the silver glow of dawn
Enriched by coruscations from the storm
Cyclonic, intensifying as to spawn
A fiery convulsion, pronged within the swarm
Of wind and dust and cresting wave
Neath flash-candescent rain, cloud, squalls
Sculpting o'er land a watery grave,
Torrential carved, extending toward sea:
Each billow rebounds as it sprawls
Clasping the shore wretched with debris,
And phantomlike recedes unto its destiny.

Life's chronicle whose evolution stretches
Through geologic time, finds disarray;
Tempestuous reels its theme which, branching, sketches
The veil of self-awareness underway—
A phantasm ambivalent o'er the wind
Is wafted unto dreamy shores,
As storms unravel and rescind
The plight that compasses desire.
Tranquility again restores
Emotive beauty—a rainbow to inspire
Transcendence of passion through nature's atmospheric lyre.

GEYSER

Upwelling violent, and falling is the geyser
Whose deep, magmatic chambered energizer
In vaporous spasms, superheated expands
Mid torrid rock and pressures it withstands
For periodic bursts from hidden springs
Seething, pulsing from a reservoir:
Volcanic in origin, it seismic clings,
Stratified in rock or vast seashore
Transformed by time, tectonic plate revival,
Toward fountains issuing fervent in arrival.

Subterranean water, volcanic fire
Spawn thunderous geysers scalding o'er the mire
Cratered in mud, bubbling, scouring with passion
Surrounding land that lava flows would fashion,
As life bears legacy through algal types,
A panoply of color o'er thermal change,
Clustering, binding hot springs with mineral stripes
When blue-green yields to rust at cooler range.
The eruptive cycle acts as synthesizer
With rain and heat transfigured into a geyser.

VOLCANO

Encircled by clouds writhing neath a void
Expansive, born of heavenly light and mists,
The mountains fume in rhythms unalloyed
By man and his vainglory. Air exists
In heated splendor, pressured by winds upsurging
While life abides mid fates of doom converging.

The summits pinnacled in fervor stand,
Rising mystical from out the sea,
And radiantly sunbeams diffuse o'er land
Tectonic fashioned, clothed in greenery;
While blanching, cloaked in haze upon ascent,
A lofty vision stirs, by nature lent.

As sculptors of landforms, sea and atmosphere,
Subduction trenches, rift zones with upwelling
Magma, interweave a chandelier
Of lava fountains, sprays—the fire propelling
In spasms, frenetic eruptive tracery
Neath ash clouds thundering and infernal free.

Volcanic wind, incineration, steam
O'er fiery ringlets veil the devastation;
Convulsing paroxysmal, gases stream
From tentacles of lava concentration
Upon escarpments, as quiescent lakes
Mirror the ash mid onset of earthquakes.

Expansive roils the pyroclastic flow,
Acidic is the avalanche of fire
With clouds sulphureus billowing mid glow
Silhouetted on the sky. Such ire
Of nature heals with soil fecundity,
And smoldering are colors of setting sun o'er sea.

The cycle of restoration and renewal
Following trauma or adversity,
Releases, from a lifetime of accrual,
A seismic strength impassioned by destiny;
And magisterial, like the realm volcanic,
The heart emblazoned, upwells with love titanic.

TREES

The trees in towering waves encompass time
With seasonal records woven of annual rings,
Perchance distended, narrow: a paradigm
To climate and intensity upsprings,
Varied mid light, dark, fire, rain, volcanism
And human factors, an interventional schism.

The trees, deciduous or evergreen,
Are hardwoods, softwoods and varieties
That dwell mid hills, savanna, or ravine,
Sweeping from tropics toward the temperate seas:
Each niche, crafted by time, reflects a change
From species culled, subsumed into a range.

In flowering tree with insect pollinator
Or cycad, conifer wind fertilized,
Diversity is grandest near the equator
As colors, intertwining, are harmonized,
Contrasting with the waterfall and sky,
From tallest to the gnarled, timeworn bonsai.

The pathway to renewal follows fire,
The sculptor of the forest canopy:
From ghostly embers, extinguishing, seeds spire
And resonate through time with destiny
Transfigured by fates, which the winds appease
In swells o'er waters, or whispering through the trees.

HONEYBEES

Through vast meridian of blue serene
O'erspreading forest and outstretched ravine,
Vibrations rise through fields amid the breeze,
And dithyrambic spun, the honeybees
Dispersed from hive, sing in sibilation,
Erratic bound, vanishing through air
Till sudden espied, enraptured, in exultation
They plunge toward flowers luxuriant and fair,
Blissful in hues and fragrances windblown,
And nectar hypnotic veiled in overtone.

Circumfused amidst the blossoms, each bee
Whirring, patterns an embroidery
Woven of buds. And pollen is suspended
As rhythmic, orange and yellow grains are blended.
Harmonious is return unto the tree,
Fissured by lightning midway o'er the trunk,
And murmuring deep extends the colony
Where honeycombed, the progeny are sunk.
And over time, will generations swarm
Cyclonic, animated like a storm.

AS I STAND

As I stand at the end of life, my thoughts embrace
The nebulous veil of night in colors sublime,
Phantasmagoric, dimming as they race
Accelerating toward the mortal climb
Unto eternity, where space and time
Expand as nothingness, a nihilism;
Fanciful, deceptive, this paradigm
Dissolves the imagery from out life's prism,
With spectrum of the mind, a blurring unto abysm.

Resplendent was the moonbeam long ago,
Mid panoply of stars o'er summer's eve,
Encompassing, casting the heavens in sapphire glow.
And tender, inspired by light, did I conceive
In youth a strategy, unleashed to cleave
The shadowy yoke of loneliness o'er the heart
Which isolated, uncertain of life, did grieve
For consummate rays of wisdom to impart
An equanimity, forged of science and art.

Divine was love, intense as morning sun
Revolving in flames across the azure dome;
I remember the rapture, harmony begun
As rhythmic our heartbeats, like a metronome,
Augmented life's pace; ecstatic did we roam,
Uniting with mankind compassionately,
To cherish this world, a fragile, pristine home
Ever more beautiful, as liberty
Unto all things extended, with birth of legacy.

As I stand at the end of life, pervasive is sadness
Effacing the triumph of love's panegyric,
For brief the moments stir, perchance with madness:
My thoughts grow vague; there seems an atmospheric
Haziness as notions stream chimeric,
Mingling with shadows, and decelerating;
And youth's tonalities, so wondrous, lyric,
Recede, into the harrowing maelstrom, abating
As I ascend, disembodied, contemplating,

But lo! Such phantasm vanishes abrupt!
They're gone: the shadows, images, the dream!
'Twas but a vision which, frenzied, did interrupt
Reality, cast in nightmarish gleam
Fantastical, detached, as to blaspheme
An insight, the essence of my sanity.
And inspiration, rare as the rich sunbeam,
Endures, summoned by fate's illusive key
Rewinding the chimes of life, sounding to destiny.

PHANTASY

Morn is blazoned as vast auroral gems—
With ethereal lights in airy diadems
Circling mountain, stream and waterfall
Mid sunbows, swirls of mists, whose rising sprawl
Uplifts through radiance the impassioned heart.
Divine, the light of heaven is unsurpassed
When love, compassion, mid its colors impart
A visionary realm of dreams, amassed
Emblazoned within, illimitable and free,
And voluptuous veiled with rhythms of phantasy.

As noontide spreads its pinnacles of light
Azure tincturing the vaporous height,
Birds in rich ensembles soaring high,
Entangled gladsome, gleam across the sky
With swells of music modulating clear
Harmonic through wind beneath the cloudless veil,
Serene and far, till sound waves disappear.
And twilight stirs, awaiting the nightingale,
As patterns interweave an afterglow:
Airy, seraphic born its colors flow.

'Tis night upon the lake whose placid mirror
Ripples with faint, insouciant stars, till clearer
Is calm reflected through atmospheric still.
And languishing are moonbeams o'er the hill,
While skyward arching as a tracery,
That dreamlike surge of luminescent rays,
Resplends the Milky Way: a galaxy
Inimitably o'ersprinkled with lights ablaze,
Depicting the birthplace of our Earth and sun
Where fanciful through time had life begun.

RISE OF THE AURORA

Nightfall over autumn's veil is cast,
Configured in starry silence; the heavens contrast
Infernal dark with twilight as it streams
Vaporous departing through haze and pale moonbeams,
Devoid of color. Day's transfiguration,
Wrought of light and harmony of hues,
Has passed. And distant is the constellation
A stellar fashioned, atmospheric ruse
Exotic arrayed as drama through the night,
Immersed in dreams deceptive taking flight.

Aye! Across a vast and airy expanse
Of Nordic bleakness, phantasms assume a trance
Which, vacillating, coldly luminescent,
Spires above the gloom in waves tumescent
As errant and rhythmic, night's heart tones abound
In spectral images; 'tis like the mind
When tortured nightmarish through anguish; 'twould resound
In shrieks, spasmodic with sanity confined
To evanescence of notions interspersed
With rarest of colors, a volatile outburst!

AURORAL PHANTASM

Phantasmal arrays of light-beams seething, shimmering
As apparitions, shower across the night,
Pulsing bizarre, surrealistic glimmering,
Expansive, panoramic in their plight.
A magnetic maze of atmospheric light
Writhing, with distortions rarefied,
Tenuous clings while rippling like a blight,
And compasses the solar wind and tide
In undulating flourish, till polar rays subside.

Would dreaming in color deceptive consummate
Such aberrant veiled, phantasmagoric trance?
Subconscious and sophistic stirs the fate
Fantastical, when fearful tones enhance
An imagery eccentric, forged by chance
Unbridled, grotesque along a deviant path
Diverging formless toward a wide expanse
When sudden! A harrowing and nightmarish wrath
Surrenders consciousness—a thralldom in aftermath.

STORM AND EMOTION

Exotic cloud forms obliterate light,
Swirling and writhing on currents of air
Like spirits evolving from a nightmare
With incantation, diaphanous flight:
Frenetic ascending in ghostly quest,
Portentous depicted are whirlwinds of fear
Capping the thunderheads bleak coalesced
From darkness clustered abysmal, austere:
Lowering, in protean veil disguised,
Clouds like emotions are quick energized.

The drama of Earth contending with sky
Is cyclic: from lightning streaking in pulses
To darkness pervasive. Again, there convulses
A cloudscape, spasmodic, flashing o'er high;
With rarefied gases and whorls of dust,
A cyclone presides, shifting in mood
And rhythm, accelerating wind gust.
Such feverish swells through high altitude
Expose instability man must endure
From storms raging inward, disease without cure.

Altruistic, reciprocal, mankind abides
As responses are moulded from incoming cues;
One defends his truth and subverts a ruse;
This erratic, self-lauding temperament guides:
Like weather inclement, subjective impression
Bewitchingly storms, impugning such facts,
Defensive denied, as guilt and transgression:
Emotion unbridled like wind interacts,
When our minds, the tempests interred, contravene
The forces behind a group's changeable mien.

LOVE DEPARTED

Alone and dark the world is unto me
As tones are cadenced in a minor key
With dirge and lamentation to impart
Despondency dysrhythmic in my heart.

Yet nature pulses through the night in glee
With starlight metrical upon the sea
Exuberant to shore with billowed flow
Beyond, where Earth lies comforted with snow.

And shadows frolicking neath frosted trees,
Loom defiant as my heart decrees
A melancholy still when love has died,
Its splendor nevermore to be espied.

Deprived of love, a rhythmic fount recedes
As ravaged, the heart in isolation bleeds,
Exuding, while phantoms fill the chambered core,
Pulsating dissonant till heard no more.

SLEEP

When sleep entwines with dark to close the path of day,
The glow from phantasy's eidolon cloaks the mind,
Whose stormy matrix swells impassioned as thoughts stray
In aberrant guise, the dreams which fancifully may find
An equilibrium lost within subconsciousness.
The trance is likened to a ravaged mountain top,
Where lightning leaps from clouds convulsing in distress
As one contends with tempests in a rage nonstop.
Then quaintly, fear and phantasmagoria are sequestered,
And placid shine the stars on panoramic peaks,
Where man alone with nature's forces stands unfettered
Portraying that elusive destiny he seeks.
The orb of day now casts a light from out the deep,
Igniting consciousness above horizoned sleep.

SPIRIT

I am the spirit of the cosmic sea,
And rule the universe star showered in fire,
With tentacles of streaming rays, that free
The orbs from dark and nurture life's desire.

I spun the galaxies' magnetic maze,
And threaded light through curvature of time
And space, with gyres of interstellar haze
Embosomed in a mathematic chime.

My heartbeat spawned the moment of creation,
My pulse ignites the supernova burst,
Yet fated is a lifeless desolation
When I depart, with darkness then dispersed.

AT THE WINDOW

Gathering at the window, mid the dews
And shadowy breath of morn, lightrays diffuse
And limn rejuvenation neath sunrise
Crimson blushed, yet azuring the skies.
Oneiric mood embraces the expanse,
With resurrection of lost love or hope;
Chromatic tones, like brainwaves from a trance,
Configure to phantasms blazoned on the cope:
Such omnitude of images at dawn
Is cadenced as emotion, life's portrait drawn.

At the window is a glass partition
Clear, reflective, like an apparition—
The veil tween life and death, past and future,
Whose phantom threads, plaited by time, would suture
The fabric of reality: 'tis strange,
As hologram it binds the universe,
Encoding all such information, change—
A semblance fundamental to disperse
Nature's laws; like mirrored, flowing glass,
'Tis vague, deceptive, a fanciful impasse.

SUSTAINMENT

'Tis midnight among the resonant peaks,
Where snowflakes are flung into wind woven streaks
That glisten beneath the star showered field,
The Milky Way's wreath intertwiningly sealed
Surrendering dark sky where spirits may reign,
And hence comets fly with mysterious train
Or asteroids plunge from mystic induction,
And feverish expunge, in demonic destruction,
A tenuous life on planets unknown
Where chaos is rife in domains like our own.

But now must mankind abolish this presence
Through puissance of mind, with internal coalescence
And quaking of fire, spasmodic within,
The passion and ire whose reverberant din
Convulses the vessels' blood-mounting wave,
That through the heart wrestles pulsatingly brave,
Surmounting the wraiths' illusory veil
While flooding our faith's optimistic regale.

Yet shadows ascending, nebulous wrought,
Confuse the forfending of specters distraught,
And clashing of boughs from trees iced below,
Portentous avows a resurgence of woe.

But list to the calm extending toward sky,
The firmament's balm as a blessing o'er high
Angelically sprinkling radiance as fair
As star clustered twinkling inspiring a prayer:

"All heavenly light diaphanous rayed
Transfixes a blight as its pangs are waylaid,
Celestially cleansing sinister forces
Whose vapors condensing pervade human sources."

With harmony dwelling over the spheres,
The quest for the quelling of evil uprears,
And vigilance bound intense with aversion
May shriekingly sound with a strident dispersion
Of recondite forms eternal assailing
Theses summits with storms, intermittent prevailing.

RHYTHMS IN THE FOREST

Expanses of isolation, loneliness
Are unified through tones as life resounds:
Songbirds resonating soft caress
The layered canopies with nesting mounds,
Through cadences of courtship. A species abounds
In rhythmic modes, fine-tuned throughout the ages,
Protective of small fledglings o'er the grounds,
Or one airborne who rapid disengages
A course, instilling fear its parent quick assuages.

And cloudbursts, rains and waterfalls renew
Entangled viridescence, effulgent flowers,
Whose ghostly patterns writhe amid the dew,
Defining, in perspective, their hazy bowers
Enfolding neath skies, configured o'er trees, watchtowers
For birds of prey, clustering toward rapid dive:
Sequenced like lightning prongs, each raptor o'erpowers
Its quarry; encumbered, they toward the nests arrive
Fatigued, and yet another day their young survive.

Survival designates success through time
As life-forms mid neutrality enlist
From nature, conditions unique unto each clime.
And ever changing, modified, exist
The wrathful atmospheric rain and mist
From tempests in frenetic swirled assault.
Intense, brief, violent cataclysms consist
Of cleansing, from land and sea to heavenly vault,
Followed by calm and nurture, rhythms to exalt.

ATMOSPHERIC CONFIGURATION

From sunrise to setting sun with green flash, streams
The atmosphere; and protean it gleams
As aerial enfolding masses cluster
And volatile, tonalities of luster,
Transfigured through optics, chromatic blend as hues
Of solar halos, mock suns, or sun pillars;
Perchance coronas, glories, may diffuse:
The vapors and ice crystals are distillers
Of light, voluptuous, fantastical:
Illusions the atmosphere would vast corral.

With sun and rain clouds mystically arrayed
In evanescent, intricate cascade,
The rainbow arched concentrically transcends
As lyrical, prismatic light extends
In rarefaction; mirror imaged and bright,
Coupled, with colors reversed, a pair, serene
Across a rainfall, assumes its wayward flight,
Hoisted o'er hills or waters of aquamarine;
'Tis majesty suspended like a trance,
Gliding through time in atmospheric romance.

As day is seized by night's fecundity
And surmounted by shadows born of phantasy;
Paroxysmal rises a ghostly glimmer,
The northern lights, awakening, writhe and shimmer
Through chilling air; sustained is luminescence
Mutable, entwined and indistinct;

Above, the patterns ripple in quiescence,
Like phantoms locked within a dream and linked
Precarious, vacillating unto time:
And shades erode, distant in their climb.

'Tis past; with morning folded in loveliness
Pristine, no trace remains of night's distress.
Sunrays intensifying, gloss the trees
Till spangled in gold are swaying canopies.
Refreshed is life within its matinal dream:
Woven into the wind gusts harmonizing,
Is floral sweetness midst a color scheme
From songbirds, winging through azure depths, chastising
The interplay of life forms round the nests:
And in sublimity the daytime rests.

HARP I

Textured with ancient motifs, a pillar rises
Supporting the harp and its harmonic curve;
Bisected by strings, the soundboard symbolizes
A resonance, chromatic compassing verve,
Tonality our minds inspired preserve
For solitude divine upon the day.
And gusts of phantom winds through strings may swerve
Modulating wave forms whose array,
Reverberant with bliss, would air a roundelay.

Augustly featured, pristine the strings resound
When pedals forge the heptatonic scale
As once or twice depressed, new tones abound.
Such double action, exquisite in detail,
Yields subtle overtones that sweet regale
The atmosphere, cadenced in strains of old:
As songs caressed by dreams create portrayal
Resplendent as the artistry of gold,
Sanctified by love's concordance to behold.

Through nature's bowers with songbirds on the wing,
Or beauty of each life's tonalities,
The harp resounds across primordial spring,
When floral motifs, amid the rain and breeze,
Transcend revitalized o'er lands and seas.
Such visions revered through time may evanesce,
Though puissance of mind, resurgent by degrees,
Resurrects such themes to effloresce,
Harmonious as the harp, where dreams rich coalesce.

HARP II

Gilt in ancient motifs, the harp consists
Of pillar, harmonic curve, ornate sound board
With strings whose compass diagonal exists
As rising diatonics in accord.
With seven foot pedals, chromatics are underscored
Till all the major and minor scales are born
With modulations intricate outpoured
Dreamlike o'er quiescence of the morn
Which crystalline harmonics, octaves above, adorn.

Well-tempered, voluptuous sounds the harp of gold
As glissandos in rapid pulses harmonize
With sequences of overtones extolled.
A cadenza, rhapsodic in tempo, diversifies
Cadenced in trills, airs, strains to improvise,
Matching springtime glory and sweetness in swells
And melodic veiling fantastical sunrise
Whose color motif like tonal splendor dwells
Deep within the heart, where loveliness upwells.

Angelic fashioned is the resonance
With rippling, crescendo of arpeggios,
Ornament and metrics that enhance
The rhythms of spring, when blossoms of the rose
Or floral rejuvenation and repose
Are tuned like harp strings mellowed with a theme.
'Tis nature's variation that bestows
Life's melodies amid the bright sunbeam,
Coordinating beauty with colors from a dream.

PROGRESSION

The United States with world hegemony
Confronts such countries, vile with exploitation
Diffuse, intense, from sociopathy
Internal bred mid death, severe privation,
Shackling of free will, as liberation
Like a phantom cloistered in the mind,
Episodic stirs o'er desolation,
Inciting wrath and overtones defined
As democratic voices, rapid suppressed, maligned.

Throughout history, empires sudden rise
Yet rule imperious with a common fate
Of fragmentation, ultimate demise.
Allegiances, ephemeral, dissipate
Within a stoic, totalitarian state
With visions, bleak in economic plight
When organized insidious to create
Assent, robotic unity and might
That militarily reigns, a dictatorial blight.

Pollution, poisons, proliferation in arms
Resound mid human rights atrocities,
And frequent coal-fired nuclear plant that harms
Environments across all lands and seas.
Rapacious decimation to appease
Officials, rends the world resolve and trade
Toward evil, manufactured as disease:
A bankrupting, computer hacking raid
O'ertakes the free-world's jobs, with ethics quick waylaid.

Through trade, production grows toward specialization
As oversight and focus on detail
Allow consumption with diversification
When cultures, intermingling, quell betrayal
And forge a trust to overcome travail.
Humanity as species must assure
That through exchange and mutual timescale,
A compromise, upsurging, would endure
With quality assurance toward expenditure.

FAME

Conquering volatile heights, lofty, free,
Defines the momentary sweep of fame,
Wherein a loss of anonymity
Erodes the luster compassing one's name;
Yet lo! Intemperate flares such vile acclaim,
Pompous, vacuous as adulation
Lionizing dominion like a flame,
Which deep within the heart sparks ruination
When ruling as pinnacle of public expectation.

And specious identities o'ertake life's sphere
Diverging wretched, lost beneath light rays
With baleful distortions, nightmarish and austere.
Yet as the mind awakens from a daze,
Ambivalent, it stormily inveighs
Against a futile, linear procession—
As time, its meaning, spinning out of phase,
Transmogrify neath sun into depression
Dark as suicide, a poignant last discretion.

DAMN THE DEA

Barbarism rules the DEA,
Collective brain bulk of a PEA,
As prohibition toward the opioid
Empowers politics with paranoid
And sanctimonious vice, whose creed is void:
"No pain, no gain," so patients suffering pray
For suicide, the DEA cachet.

The senseless war on drugs creates the thugs,
Cartels financed by Uncle Sam's humbugs,
A government industry; 'tis all in vain:
The psychedelics, crime and masses slain,
Despite the politicians' dire campaign
'Bout "God We Trust" and patriotic plugs—
All misguided mid Congressional lugs.

BEREAVEMENT

Metamorphosis, mid sun and rain
Reflective, streaming, obfuscates our loss
Bound by time whose intermittent pain
Dwells deep, haunting within—a specious gloss
Of healing mid uncertainties that toss
The mind. Bereavement lingers ill-defined
'Tween phantasy, reality; across
A chasm ghostly visions rise entwined,
Distending open wounds, mantled with thoughts maligned.

Yet vaporous is morn o'erspread upon the mountains,
Unveiling light expressive of desire
And love, whose resurrection like great fountains
Upwells through haze to atmospheric inspire
Blushing of dawn o'er empyreal sapphire.
For passionate the heart's ethereal tones,
Like music born angelic from the lyre,
Or light cast luminous through rare gemstones,
Would harmonize enriched, mid nature's healing zones.

SPRINGTIDE*

'Tis warm amid the glorious rites of spring
When opulent blows the yellow jessamine
Entwining; from dormancy the tendrils cling
Ascending in blossoms, fragrant and crystalline,
Fervent toward clouds enfolded o'er aquamarine.
And winds from land, sea, heaven's sphere circling rise
Integrating colors, vast, pristine,
As waters shine and visionary skies
Transfigure light of day, a celestial enterprise.

And blossoms are suffused through afterglow
Diaphanous, divine with glossy tint,
Ephemeral in the strangeness of its flow
Dappled as diversified imprint
Upon life's splendor: like sparks when struck from flint,
Amassing radiance and bathed within a glaze
Reflected from water to sky in colorful glint,
Subtle mid contrasting of sunrays
Rejuvenating dreams, with passing of our days.

*To my wife, Deidra—through the
seasonal felicity of springtide,
may the Carolina yellow jessamine
instantiate the loveliness of your
existence.

CLOUDS

Clustering like a vast enfolded quilt,
Clouds contrast upon the sapphirine
O'erflowing with tresses, soft, flocculent built
And tousled by wind while billowing pristine
Immense across the azure crystalline—
A scaffolding of beauty, outspreading dreams
That bind with love upon an airy demesne
Lit by the meridian orb in rich light-beams
Ornamenting life mid nature's enraptured themes.

Clouds reflect, like facets of a gem,
The intricacies of phantasy and mood,
That mould the mind like a diadem
Whose emotional jewels resplend in solitude,
Ephemeral, fathomless, artful and oft endued
With constructs compassing the universe
As theories of reality construed;
Till thought, like clouds; its images disperse,
Dissolving into dreams, wherein our hearts immerse.

Printed in the United States
By Bookmasters